The Witch-Finder General vs. the Firebrand-Darlings

By CL Gammon

I0162067

𝒟ℛℬ

Deep Read Press

LAFAYETTE, TENNESSEE

www.deepreadpress.com

Manufactured in the United States of America

ISBN: 978-1-954989-19-1 (Paperback)

ISBN: 978-1-954989-20-7 (Hardback)

Copy Edited By: Kim Gammon

Cover Design by: Kim Gammon

Published by:

DEEP READ PRESS

Lafayette, Tennessee

www.deepreadpress.com

This book is for all those who recognize injustice and choose to fight against it.

Books by CL Gammon

The Witch-Finder General vs. the Firebrand-Darlings is the sixth book on the persecution of accused witches written by CL Gammon. The other five are:

A Laughing Witch: Hanging Susannah Martin

Dixie Witches: 9 True Southern Witch Trials

Salem Sends Its First Witch to the Gallows

The Queen and King of Hell in Salem

The Witches of Salem, In Their Own Words

You can find them all and many other books by CL Gammon at amazon.com or at the Deep Read Press website, www.deepreadpress.com

The biblical verses quoted in this book are from the King James Version and are in the public domain.

The images used in this book are in the public domain.

Table of Contents

Introduction

THIS small volume takes a fresh look at England's "Witch-finder General," Matthew Hopkins. It traces his short, sorted life, and discusses the pain and death he caused to hundreds and the fear he evoked in thousands of others.

The reign of Hopkins as England's most prolific persecutor of witches although brief, was terrible. Yet, he felt no guilt from his crimes. On the contrary, he expressed pride in them and defended them before the world.

This book concentrates on the justifications Hopkins gave for his blatant violation of British law in the pursuit of witches during his short witch-finding career. He also defended the exorbitant fees he charged communities for his dubious services.

The first section of this volume traces his defense. It also reveals how his methods served, at least in part, as the inspiration for later witch-hunts.

The second section covers in brief detail some of the tools Hopkins used. It also covers some of the topics touched on in this book.

The third section deals with the Devil, how the Puritans viewed him, and what the Bible says about him.

Speaking of the Bible, the author quotes hundreds of biblical passages taken from the

King James Version. The Puritans employed the King James Version and it is only fitting that the quotes used here come from it.

The author hopes that the life and misdeeds of Matthew Hopkins will serve as a cautionary tale. We must always be alert to the designs of unscrupulous men who, if left encumbered, would exercise their power to abuse the weak and defenseless.

SECTION I: THE DEFENSE

THIS Section deals with how Matthew Hopkins defended his witch-finding career. One must remember that it is his account supported by nothing but his word.

1. Hopkins Finds Witches

MATTHEW HOPKINS,
OF MANNINGTREE, ESSEX,
THE CELEBRATED WITCH-FINDER.
FROM A VERY RARE PRINT IN THE PEPYSIAN LIBRARY, AT
MAGDALENE COLLEGE, CAMBRIDGE.

MATTHEW Hopkins was born around 1620 in Great Wenham, Suffolk, England. In his twenty-seven or so years, he earned eternal infamy for persecuting those he accused of being witches. Even though his career was short and his area of operation limited,

Hopkins was Britain's most prolific and notorious witch-finder.

Few documents exist that shed light on his early life. However, there is some information about Matthew Hopkins. He grew up in Wenham, Suffolk. He was the fourth son of six children born to James Hopkins. James Hopkins was a devout Puritan and he served as Vicar of St. John's Church in Wenham. James Hopkins was very popular among his large flock of parishioners.

Matthew's sibling, John, was also a clergyman. He was the Minister of the Church of Fambridge, but church leaders removed him because he was lazy and he neglected his work.

The Hopkins family had been wealthy in years past. At one point, they owned "lands and tenements in "Framlingham at the castle." James Hopkins was not as rich as earlier family members had been, but he had enough wealth when he died in 1634 to leave his heirs goodly sums of about £100 each.

In the early 1640s, Matthew Hopkins moved the approximate ten miles from Wenham to Manningtree, Essex. In Manningtree, he used his inheritance to purchase a nice home. In addition, he purchased a tavern called the Thorn Inn in nearby Mistley.

Hopkins may have been a trained attorney, although there are no documents proving it. The way Hopkins handled himself in a court of law indicated that he might have had a legal background. Trained attorney or not, he knew his way around a courtroom.

The Witch-Finder General

Hopkins began his witch-finding career in March 1644 and he retired in 1647. Hopkins and his team began their witch-finding activities in the region now called "East Anglia" (Suffolk, Essex, Norfolk, Cambridgeshire, and Huntingdonshire counties) and then he expanded their operations to the counties of North Hamptonshire and Bedfordshire. Hopkins operated during the English Civil War and his territory was under the tight control of Cromwell's Parliamentary Army. Hopkins and his "witch prickers" never ventured into areas under the control of Charles I. This simple fact leads to the assumption that there was a political component to the witch-hunts.

Hopkins and his little band of witch-finders did not have the official sanction of Cromwell or of Parliament. Yet, Cromwell, himself a devout Puritan, had to be aware that Hopkins was ferreting out suspected witches. Cromwell also had to know that Hopkins had assumed the title of "Witch-Finder General." Far from trying to stop him, the authorities seemed to validate Hopkins. They issued him and his team letters of safe conduct so that they could travel from town to town unhindered.

While Hopkins was not the first English witch-finder, nor the last, he was the most prolific. During his brief career, he and his team were responsible for as many as 300 executions of accused witches. In fact, more accused witches died at his hands than suffered execution during in entire history of England before he appeared on the scene. Most of those executed on his word were women, but as many as 75 men suffered hanging on his testimony as well.

Hopkins was self-important and arrogant. His delusions of grandeur grew to the point that he christened himself "Witch-finder General" of all of England. It was not a true political title and no leader or governmental agency bestowed it upon him. Neither did his scope encompass all of England. The title was not even unique to Hopkins. Several persons called themselves Witch-finder General. However, Hopkins cemented the title by the sheer number of persons executed on his testimony.

Hopkins experienced greater success than other English witch-finders did. One reason for this was that he enjoyed certain advantages that other witch-finders did not have. Hopkins was active during the long and bloody civil war between forces loyal to King Charles I and Parliamentary forces under the direction of Oliver Cromwell. It was an unsettled time and men like Hopkins thrive in unsettled times.

Another reason for the success Hopkins enjoyed was his passion for his work. He was cold, ruthless, sadistic, ambitious, and devoid of compassion. He may have been sociopathic as well. Perhaps most importantly, Hopkins was aggressive in his pursuit of witches. He would go to almost any extreme, including blatant violations for British law, to obtain a conviction.

Hopkins did not see his job as one of proving that any accused witch had committed any particular crime or offense. He did not even concern himself with proving that accused witches had ever practiced the black arts. His interest was in proving that the accused had entered into a covenant with the Devil. If there was no evidence of a pact with the Devil, the accused witch was a mere criminal, like any other lawbreaker. However, proof that the accused had made a compact with the Devil raised the witch to a different level of evil. In the minds of the fearful and superstitious citizens of the towns Hopkins visited, such a covenant justified immediate execution.

In continental Europe, authorities routinely applied the rule of *crimen exceptum* to witches. *Crimen exceptum* was intended to allow courts to waive the ordinary rules of justice in exceptional cases. By proving the accused had made a pact with the Devil, authorities could declare that witches had committed the exceptional crime of heresy against the church, and apply *crimen exceptum*. Thus, witches were subject to torture and other forms of brutality during interrogations. In addition, courts could convict witches without any physical evidence at all.

In England, it was technically illegal for witch-finders to employ physical torture to obtain confessions from suspected witches. However, leaders did not generally attempt to prevent Hopkins from abusing those he suspected. One reason for this was that the authorities supported Hopkins in his efforts to eradicate witches, and they largely ignored his illegal methods. Another reason was that Hopkins intimidated local authorities. They feared that if they interfered with him too strongly, he would accuse *them* of being witches.

2. Opposition to Hopkins

EVENTUALLY, Hopkins and his obnoxious band of witch-finders began to face opposition to their work. One important opponent of the witch-finders was John Gaule, Vicar of Great Staughton in Huntingdonshire. In 1646, Gaule interviewed a woman from St. Neots that authorities had jailed until Hopkins could get there and perform various witch tests upon her. The poor woman's condition after days of maltreatment in jail appalled Gaule.

The news that Gaule had interviewed the woman worried Hopkins. He feared that the townsfolk would be inclined to reject his determination that the woman was a witch. Hopkins had sent members of his team ahead to stir up witch fever in the town. Before coming himself, he wrote a letter to an ally asking if he would get a "good welcome" when he arrived to test the woman.

Gaule did not believe the poor jailed woman had committed any crime. Beyond that, the fact that Hopkins would not visit a town unless promised a "good welcome" angered the Vicar. Gaule immediately penned a pamphlet titled, *Select Cases of Conscience touching Witches and Witchcrafts*. Attempting to enlist important help, Gaule dedicated the pamphlet to Colonel Valentine Walton, a member of the British House of Commons. Additionally, Gaule gave a series of Sunday sermons aimed at suppressing witch hunting.

The opposition to Hopkins, especially the complaints to his torturing the accused and charging massive fees for his services, grew rapidly. Finally, the Court of Assizes at Norfolk called him to testify before it.

The justices stated that many had been condemned and executed on the word of Hopkins, and it was likely that he intended to condemn others. The judges held that questioning him was necessary because, "Life is precious and there is need of great inquisition before it is taken away."

One of the answers the judges wanted answered was why vast majority of those Hopkins accused were "silly Women that know not their right hands from their left." "Why," the judges wondered, "did the Devil confine himself to enlisting poor old women into his service?"

The next several chapters contain the responses Hopkins made to this and the other questions the judges put before him. Additionally, the next several chapters contain other related material.

3. Was Hopkins a Witch?

THE judges reasoned that only "the greatest witch, sorcerer, of wizard" could have exposed so many witches in such a short period as did Hopkins. They asked him if that wasn't so.

Hopkins scoffed at the idea that he was a witch. He paraphrased the Bible in his defense. He asked the judges, "If Satan's kingdom be divided against itself, how can it stand?"

The reference Hopkins made was from Matthew 12:26 when Jesus asked, "And if Satan cast out Satan, he is divided against himself; how shall then his kingdom stand?"

Of course, the verse Hopkins paraphrased had nothing to do with finding witches.

There were plenty of biblical verses that Hopkins could have applied which spoke of witchcraft (See Chapters 16 and 29 for biblical references to witchcraft.)

4. Hopkins and the Devil

SOME of the judges believed that the only explanation for the success Matthew Hopkins enjoyed in finding witches was that he had met with the Devil and had received the book the Evil One carried containing all the names of England's witches. In addition, some judges conjectured that the Devil had given Hopkins the power to discern witches by their facial expressions.

Hopkins denied he had received the Devil's Book. However, he continued that if he had outsmarted the Devil and gotten the book, it would be a "great commendation, and no disgrace at all."

Hopkins also denied that he had any special means to determine a witch through a suspect's facial expression. He stated that he discovered witches from the tried and true methods he employed and not by any magical means. (For more on the Devil's Book see Chapter 17.)

5. Hopkins and His Abilities

THE judges wondered where Hopkins had gained the skill to locate so many witches so quickly and with such apparent ease. They asked Hopkins if he had achieved this witch finding ability from "profound learning" acquired from reading the works of previous witch-hunters.

Hopkins responded that his abilities came not from books, but from experience alone. He claimed that experience was the "surest and safest way to judge" if someone was a witch. However, Hopkins had consulted witch-hunting manuals. In later testimony, he quoted from a book by King James VI of Scotland, and I of England, called, *Daemonologie*.

Later witch-hunters relied on more than their own experiences. They studied the writings of Hopkins and others witch-finders in their attempts to locate guilty parties. (For a look at witch hunting guides, see Chapter 18.)

6. Learning His Trade

SINCE Hopkins contended that he derived his abilities to find witches from experience alone, the judges wondered where he had gained that experience.

Hopkins responded that he did not have to travel far to find witches. Then, he told the court of his beginnings as a witch-finder. He related that in early March 1644, he located several members of a "horrible sect of witches" living in his hometown of Manningtree. He said that these witches held meetings with witches from nearby towns every six weeks on Friday nights. (See Chapter 19 for information on Witch Sabbaths.)

Hopkins related that these witches held their Sabbaths near his home. He stated that the witches made "solemn sacrifices" to the Devil. However, he did not detail what those solemn sacrifices were. He continued that once he heard a witch speaking to her imp (familiar spirit). The witch ordered the familiar to have a conversation with another witch. This was in line with the common belief that witches sometimes used familiar spirits to communicate with each other. (See Chapter 20 for information on Familiar Spirits.)

The witch hunters apprehended the witch that had ordered her familiar to speak to another witch and had her searched by "women who had for many years known the Devil's Marks." The searchers found three nipples on the suspect where, according to Hopkins, "honest women have not" any. (See Chapter 22 for a discussion of Devil's Marks.)

According to Hopkins, the judge ordered the suspected witch kept awake until she contacted her familiars. Hopkins said that on the fourth night, the suspect could not resist any longer and finally called her familiars to her. Hopkins testified that he and nine others witnessed the witch call her familiar spirits by their names and tell them what shapes to take that evening.

Hopkins then described each of the familiars the witch called:

1. Holt was a white kitten.

2. Jarmara was a fat Spaniel without any legs.

The witch later confessed that she kept Jarmara fat by causing him to suck "good blood" from her body.

3. Vinegar Tom was like a long-legged Greyhound with a head like an ox. The familiar had a long tail and "broad eyes."

Hopkins claimed he spoke with Vinegar Tom. Hopkins said he ordered the familiar spirit "to go the place" provided for the Devil and "his angels." That is, to return to Hell. With that, Vinegar Tom transformed himself into the shape of a headless four-year-old child. The familiar then ran around the house six times and vanished.

4. Sack and Sugar was like a black rabbit.

5. Newes looked like a skunk.

Hopkins stated that all the familiar spirits disappeared soon after the accused witch called them.

Hopkins claimed that the above-mentioned accused witch confessed and that she implicated others. Upon investigation, Hopkins found a large coven of witches operating near his home. He said he proved the witches guilty by finding marks on them, and by locating their familiar spirits. The familiar spirits carried names such as "Elemanzer," "Pyewacket," "Peckin the Crown," "Grizzel," "Greedigut" and others that that Hopkins said no mortal could invent.

The witch-finder said, once proven guilty the witches confessed and confirmed what the first witch had told Hopkins even though he had not revealed what the informer had told him.

The witches admitted attending witch Sabbaths and committing heinous crimes. Hopkins bragged that he located 100 witches in Essex and that authorities condemned 29 of them immediately. Additionally, and he took four others the 25 miles to his hometown for hanging.

The Devil attempted to stop Hopkins and his with-finders, so said Hopkins. The Devil, in the form of a bear, accosted Hopkins in his garden and tried to kill him, but Hopkins survived the assault. Interestingly, although Hopkins played hero and swore that he had defeated the Devil, he did not give any details of the battle.

Although Hopkins thought highly of himself, he declared that anyone that had his experience (that is, anyone who had dealt with hundreds of witches), and his skills (his self-proclaimed genius for uncovering evildoers), could find witches as well and as easily as he did.

7. True Devil's Marks

THE last chapter went in some detail about what Devil's Marks were, what the witch-finders believed the marks to be, and how examiners tried to find them. It is apparent that the judges found the idea of Devil's Marks dubious.

The judges pointed out that older people, especially women were often "troubled" by warts, growths, and other natural marks from childbearing, hemorrhoids, farm injuries, and other conditions. They asked how Hopkins, acting alone, could possibly condemn an old man or woman for having a Devil's Mark.

Hopkins said the examiners he approved, and often brought with him from town to town, could justify their skill in identifying Devil's Marks. He continued that they could present good reasons why the marks they identified were not natural and were not the result of the conditions the judges mentioned.

Hopkins continued tat charges that only one person examined the bodies of suspected witches were "most false and untrue." The Witch-Finder General said the common practice was for a dozen or more of the "ablest men in the parish" to appoint a number of "skillful" older women to take part in the examination. Hopkins implied that these women had previous experience in examining accused witches. However, he didn't elaborate on their experience.

Hopkins related that the authorities then put accused witches on trial based on the examination by the skilled matrons, and not by *his* testimony concerning any Devil's Marks.

The fact was that the matrons examined the accused based on the charges Hopkins made. The examiners felt duty bound to find some kind of lesion, dry skin, birthmark, or something else that could claim was a teat. Besides that, if they found questionable marks and determined they were from the Devil they received compensation for their services.

The threat of an examination caused some confessions. The prospect of a humiliating examination was too much for some. They confessed to prevent examiners from stripping them naked and prodding and poking them for hours in a room full of people, mostly men.

Others submitted to the ordeal believing that since they were innocent, the old matrons would not find anything. Sadly, most of those accused witches that acquiesced to an examination found they were mistaken in their assumptions.

8. Applying Torture

THE judges remained unconvinced that searching the witches for Devil's Marks could accomplish anything. The judges held that it was impossible for any woman to make a correct determination based on skin blemishes. It did not matter how experienced the examiner was, she could not say that marks appearing to be completely natural were not so. The judges said that unless a witch confessed that the blemishes on her body were Devil's Marks, the examiners had to accept them as normal.

Then, the judges moved on to torture. They delivered their opinion that the confessions of accused witches resulted exclusively from the application of illegal torture. The judges then stated that a person might confess to anything to end the types of torture Hopkins applied.

Hopkins disagreed with the judges. He answered the charges in three parts:

1. He said the examiners judged blemishes by how unusual they were and by where they appeared on the accused witch's body. If marks existed far removed from where one would expect to see them, the examiners identified them as Devil's Marks. For instance, nipples between the fingers of an accused witch *had* to be Devil's Marks.

Additionally, if skin deformities could be the result of childbirth or other condition, the examiners would assume they were natural. If not, they would conclude the deformities Devil's Marks.

2. If the examiners pricked a suspected deformity with a pin, needle, or nail and the accused felt no pain, the examiners assumed it was a Devil's Mark.

Over time, witch-finders developed special tools for pricking suspect deformities on witches. (See Chapter 24 for more on pricking tools.)

3. "Variations and mutations" of deformities into several shapes confirmed they were Devil's marks.

Hopkins continued that if witches learned a witch-finder was nearby, they would try to prevent exposure of their Devil's Marks. One way they did this was by causing others to suckle their familiars for them. Sometimes, according to Hopkins, witches would force their own children to suckle the familiars. This implied that the children of witches were also witches, or that familiars could suckle from anyone, witch or not.

Without familiars suckling from them, the Devil's marks on the witch reduced in size. Soon they appeared to be nothing more than dry or hanging skin. However, if no familiar came to feed for several days, the witch's teats filled with "corruption" and extended back out to their full size. The witch would then have no

choice but to summon a familiar to feed from
her. When the familiar came, the witch-finder
would have his proof and would have no need
of torture to obtain a conviction.

9. Questions About Imps

UP to that point, the judges still doubted that Hopkins was correct in his views regarding familiar spirits (imps) suckling from the blood of witches. The judges pointed out an obvious fact: If the Devil created a spirit, the spirit would need no nourishment. Why then, would this spirit, "having neither flesh nor bone," desire to drink the blood of a witch?

Hopkins had a rationalization for this contradiction. He agreed with the judges that familiar spirits were not flesh and bone and that they did not *need* human blood for sustenance. Yet, he contended that they suckled nonetheless.

Hopkins said the non-mortal familiars suckled in order to "aggravate the witch's damnation and to put into her in mind of her Covenant" with the Devil. That is, familiar spirits humiliated witches and would not let them forget that they belonged to the Devil.

Hopkins related to the judges that familiars were spirits of the "Prince of the air" (the Devil) and could take any shape the Devil desired. It didn't matter what form familiars took, they were all the same in essence, according to Hopkins. This was a contradiction of a previous statement. Earlier, Hopkins told the court that a witch had told her familiars what form to take. Now he said that the Devil made that decision. However, Hopkins conceded that the

Devil could not create actual living, breathing creatures. God alone could do that.

Seeming to contradict himself again, Hopkins held that the spirits behaved as flesh and blood creatures would. He stated that they could actually draw blood from, and enter the bodies of witches. He continued that familiar spirits could also control the actions of their hosts, cause them to speak the Devil's words, and prevent them from quoting from the Bible.

The reasons for his contradictions in the answers Hopkins may have been honest. It is clear that Hopkins was uncertain if witches controlled their familiars, or if familiars controlled their witches.

10. More About Torture

THE judges brought up the matter of torturing witches again. They asked that when Devil's Marks were not sufficient to gain a conviction, why Hopkins found it necessary to apply exhaustion torture to suspects. Exhaustion torture included sleep depravation and "walking" witches to gain confessions. (See Chapter 26 for more about exhaustion torture.)

The judges especially objected to the practice of keeping jailed suspects under constant surveillance and "walking" them. The judges pointed out that witch-finders often make the accused walk for hours on end without rest and until their feet bled. Eventfully, the exhausted suspects broke down under the cruel torture and confessed.

On one hand, Hopkins defended the use of exhaustion torture, and on the other, he denied that he was employing it at that time. Hopkins said that early on in his witch hunting, the Magistrates in Essex and Suffolk practiced sleep depravation against accused witches.

Hopkins told the judges that keeping witches awake tended to cause them to call on their familiars for help. When the familiars came out into full view, the witch-hunters had proof positive that the accused was guilty.

Hopkins continued that witches seldom, if ever complained of loss of sleep. While he believed that the use of exhaustion torture was effective, he told the court that he had discontinued the practice after the English government forbade it. Hopkins said that sometimes witches had such "stubborn wills" that they could not sleep, even though he always "tendered and offered" it to them.

Hopkins had an excuse for walking torture too. In fact, he held that walking witches was in the best interest of the accused. Hopkins stated there was no intent to torture involved in constant surveillance. The surveillance was necessary to keep the witches walking.

During the nighttime hours, if the accused sat, went to bed, or even crouched down, the watchers made them stand up and continue walking. Hopkins continued that this was because when the watchers allowed the accused to crouch, familiars would come into the cells occupied by the accused witches. The sudden appearance of the familiars frightened the watchers. The scared watchers, often, contrary to their instructions, "misused, spoiled, and abused" the witches.

Hopkins pointed out that no one ever produced evidence that *he* had taken part in or condoned the abuse of any accused witch. In fact, his own words proved that he often approved torture and applied it.

11. Dunking Witches

NEXT, the judges brought up the brutal and dangerous practice of "dunking" suspected witches. They called the Dunking Test (also called the "Swimming Test) "abominable, inhumane, and unmerciful." The judges also pointed out that English law forbade the dunking of accused witches.

The accusation offended Hopkins. Yet, he admitted that he had dunked witches with and without evidence of Devil's Marks, or any other evidence for that matter. He also conceded that that the Devil had aided him and his witch-finding team – after a fashion – in the pursuit of discovering witches.

Hopkins made his long defense of dunking in four parts:

1. Hopkins stated that the Devil's power over witches was great and the "Evil One" could persuade them to do anything he commanded. For no other reason except for mischief, the Devil often delivered his minions to witch-finders.

Hopkins explained that the Devil sometimes called witches together and convinced them that their Devil's Marks were so close together as to make them indiscernible through examination. The Devil continued that if the witches submitted to the examinations, the court would find them not guilty and they would never fall under suspicion again.

Believing the Devil, the witches followed hiss orders and walked the ten to twelve miles to the Hopkins headquarters at Norwich. There, they volunteered to submit to various tests. Hopkins was almost gleeful as he related that twenty of the deluded volunteers were "hanged for their labour."

Hopkins related the story of one volunteer specifically. This executed man was a baker called Mr. Meggs. According to Hopkins, Mr. Meggs came seven miles to Norwich and "submitted himself voluntarily to be searched for marks which were subsequently found resulting in his execution."

The Witch-Finder General continued that 40 witches confessed that the Devil told them that if they submitted to the dunking test, they would sink and the witch-finders would clear them of wrongdoing. But when dunked, they floated back to the surface and the witch-finders adjudged them guilty.

2. Hopkins contended that prosecutors never introduced the results of dunking tests as evidence at any witch trial.

There is no record that any of the judges asked why Hopkins performed the dunking tests if he did not intend to use the results in court. Yet, it would have been an obvious question. (For more on dunking witches see Chapter 27.)

3. Although Hopkins stated previously that he had relied on his own experiences to find witches, he now quoted a book called *Daemonologie* (*Demonology*) by King James. The book stated that witches denied their baptism when they made their covenant with the Devil. The witches swore that water was the only element of baptism, as well.

When the witch-finders heaved the accused into the water, it rejected her and caused her to float back to the surface. The water then forced the witch to the shore and left her there.

4. Hopkins invited the judges to notice how witches reacted when they felt abused. If someone called them "whore" or "thief," they would "wring their hands, and shed tears in abundance." Then, they would run to the nearest Justice of the Peace and file a legal complaint.

Then Hopkins commented that when they learned authorities had charged them with the "horrible and damnable sin" of witchcraft, they revealed their "stupidity." He said that faced with accusations of witchcraft, they displayed no emotion or "let one tear fall."

Hopkins finished by saying that because of their lack of emotion when charged, dunking tests were not necessary. Of course, Hopkins contradicted himself again. He had testified earlier that he could not determine if a person was a witch based on her facial expression. Another point is that if witches did not cry when accused, there was no point in testing them at all.

12. Denying Torture

THE judges contended that Hopkins could "wring out a word or two of confession" from the "stupefied, ignorant, unintelligible, poor, silly creatures," through torture. Then, even if he was the only one who heard the confessions, he could blackmail his victims into implicating "innocent" people. The judges held that the poor tortured people understood that implicating others was the only way for them to avoid more torture and eventual hanging.

Hopkins scoffed at the idea that he put any credence into the confessions accused witches made under torture, even if they implicated no one but themselves. Hopkins continued that he had never accepted any confession gained by means of torture. Hopkins then presented his attempt to refute the charge in four points:

1. Hopkins "utterly" denied that the confession of a witch had any validity when extracted by any form of "torture or violence." Then, Hopkins contradicted himself. He would accept confessions obtained through some types of torture such as exhaustion torture, walking, or dunking, if the witch confessed again after she had gotten some rest.

2. Hopkins said he rejected confessions obtained by offering rewards for the accused. For instance, if the accuser gained a confession by saying to the suspect, "If you will confess you shall go home, you shall not go to the jail,

nor be hanged," Hopkins said he would reject the confession.

3. Hopkins related that he refused confessions that included fanciful accounts of performing impossible acts. The impossible stories he rejected included those witches flying in the air, riding on broomsticks, etc.

4. Hopkins said he rejected confessions when the accused had "words put into her mouth." That is, she answered leading questions affirmatively, but provided no details on her own. Hopkins related a typical interrogation he would consider having no force or effect:

Question: "You have four Imps have you not?

Answer: "Yes."

Question: "Did they not suck you?"

Answer: "Yes."

Question: "Are not their names so, and so?"

Answer: "Yes."

Question: "Did not you send such an Imp to kill my child?"

Answer: "Yes."

If this was the extent of the confession, Hopkins said the questioning accomplished nothing and he discounted it. He continued that he encouraged Magistrates and Judges to gather actual evidence during questioning and not to put words into the mouths of witches.

Hopkins was not being honest with the judges. Had he not accepted the validly of confessions obtained through torture, he would not have applied it.

Hopkins and the witch courts always offered benefits to those that confessed and implicated others. For instance, the witch courts seldom executed confessed witches. Additionally, when a confessed witch turned accuser, the court released from jail, treated her as a hero, and provided her other things.

Hopkins did accept claims of "impossible" acts from confessing witches. The very belief in witchcraft included accepting impossible acts. For instance, Hopkins certainly believed demonic spirits in the form of strange creatures fed off the blood of witches. What is more impossible than that?

Leading questions from witch-hunters, examiners, and judges were common practice. To deny that one accepted such testimony was simply untrue.

Even if Hopkins had been honest in his statements, few, if any, witch-finders were as gentle and understanding with accused witches as he claimed to be.

The Salem trials provide good examples of brutal interrogations of the accused and subsequent humiliating trials actually went.

There are many accounts of torture extracting confessions at Salem. One more interesting example of a somewhat typical interrogation follows. This interrogation was of two boys, but females suffered similar rough treatment.

During the trial of Martha Carrier at Salem, two of her sons, Richard (age 18) and Andrew (age 15) stood before overbearing Judge John Hathorne and answered questions. The snarling judge did not intimidate the Carrier children as he questioned them. They denied that they were witches several times. They also refused to accuse their mother of being a witch. In fact, they claimed she was in no way associated with the Devil.

A frustrated Judge Hathorne ordered Sheriff George Corwin to remove the boys from the courtroom and "put the question to them" in private. The Sheriff hustled the boys to the jail roughly. Then, he shoved them into a cell, struck them each several times, and ordered them to tell the "truth." Neither of the boys confessed. After absorbing several more blows, they still refused to give way.

Sheriff Corwin decided more drastic measures were necessary to get the answers he wanted. He ordered his deputy to bring him two long, strong ropes. Corwin took one rope, put it around Richard Carrier's neck, and cinched it tightly. He choked the boy for several seconds while demanding a confession. Richard's face turned red and then purple, but he gave no indication that he would admit to being a witch. The deputy choked Andrew in the same manner, with the same lack of results.

Sheriff Corwin knew he was getting nowhere and he did not want to kill the boys without first obtaining their confessions. He stopped choking Richard and ordered the deputy to stop choking Andrew as well.

Then Corwin moved on to the next form of barbarity. He removed the rope from Richard Carrier's neck and bound the boy's feet tightly together with one end of it. Then, he took the other end of the rope and threw it over a ceiling rafter. The deputy did the same with Andrew. Then the two men took the loose ends of the ropes and pulled them, hoisting the boys upside down into the air. The men tied off the ropes and continued to badger the dangling boys to confess their crimes.

The Carrier brothers held out for several more minutes, but then a little stream of blood began to trickle from Andrew's nose and the frightened boy, sure that he was about to die, promised that he would confess to the judges if the deputy would let him down. When Andrew broke, there was no reason for Richard to hold out any longer, and he too agreed to admit in open court that he was a witch.

The High Sheriff, clearly satisfied that he had performed his duties well, let the boys down, and then he ushered them back in front of the witchcraft judges. The bruised and battered boys carried the marks of their ordeal as they entered the courtroom. Additionally, Andrew's nose was still bleeding. If Judge Hathorne noticed, he did not care. He took their confessions as absolute truth and moved on to the next witness.

Another example of torture at Salem involved the ordeal of Giles Corey. The girls making most of the accusations at Salem implicated Corey and his wife Martha. Soon, both stood before the court accused of witchcraft. Martha Cory entered a not guilty plea and the authorities hanged her. Giles Corey, on the other hand, refused to enter a plea.

Under colonial law, the case against Giles Corey could not proceed until he entered a plea. In order to make him admit his guilt or claim he was innocent, the authorities made Corey lie on the ground face up. Then, they placed a wooden board on him and piled heavy stones on the board. Corey suffered the intense pain as the Sheriff added more and more stones. Finally, the stones crushed Corey and he died without ever making a plea.

As in England, at Salem, an accused witch could avoid hanging by accusing others. Some of the most frequent accusers, like Sarah Bibber, began making accusations to avoid the gallows.

While physical torture was common, at Salem, mental torture proved more effective. The authorities sometimes told small children that they would hang if they didn't confess. Additionally, the witch-finders let the horrified youngsters believe they could go home, if they implicated family members. The innocent children had no inkling that their confessions were sending their mothers to the gallows.

The Salem witch court routinely accepted impossible acts as real and true. Numerous confessions included accounts of riding through the air on poles, brooms, or even on the backs of flying witches to assemblies.

Not only did the judges at Salem put words in the mouths of the accused, they accepted only the one answer they demanded. There are many accounts of the judges browbeating witnesses until they got "truthful" answers. The witch judges considered a refusal to confess as proof of guilt.

13. Valid Confessions

THE next question was that if Hopkins rejected all the confessions that he claimed he did, what constituted a valid confession?

Hopkins explained that he would declare a confession valid by following the following procedure:

1. If examiners found "teats" (Devil's Marks) on a suspect, then the suspect was "sequestered" in jail. The only reason for this, according to Hopkins was to isolate her from her "old associates." That is, to keep her away from other witches.

2. Then, by "good counsel" the witch-finder brought her into a "sad condition" by making

her understand "the horribleness of her sin" and the punishment she would suffer.

3. The witch-finder would then make the witch understand the subtle malice the Devil displayed in tricking her.

4. Confronted with all this, the witch would feel "remorse and sorrow for complying with Satan so long, and disobeying God's sacred Commands."

5. The remorseful witch would then confess of her own accord without the application of any torture or intimidation toward her.

Hopkins related the contents of the average witch's confession. The witch would say when the Devil first came to her, and whether "ignorance, pride, anger, malice," or something else motivated her to accept the Angel of Darkness. She would tell the witch-finder about her conversations with the Devil. She would also describe the Devil's voice. She would say what shape the Devil was in when he visited her. She would relate the number, shapes, and names of the familiar spirits the Devil sent to her.

The witch would confess to what "mischief" she had sent the familiars out to perform. Hopkins said he would verify that the evil the witches said her familiars committed had actually taken place

After that, Hopkins said he would accept a confession as valid and recommend that the authorities hang her.

In this answer, Hopkins, as he usually did, contradicted his previous statements. He said he opposed torture, but he readily admitted that one of the first things he did with accused witches was to put them in isolation. Alone, frightened, deprived of sleep, and exhausted, it was just a matter of time before the poor wretches confessed just to end their horrible ordeal.

Confessed witches described the Devil in several ways. Some said he came to them in the form of a demon as is presented in medieval paintings. Others said he came as a "black man." Sometimes he was well dressed, sometimes naked. Sometimes he came in the image of a friend, sometimes as a stranger. Sometimes he came as a bird, horse, bear, or other animal. Other times he came as a hideous beast. Most confessed witches did agree on one thing – the Devil visited them either just before sunset, or during the nighttime hours.

With all the different versions of the Devil, a fearful person could imagine anyone or anything she came across, especially at night, was the Devil.

14. Witches and Power

The Witch No.3.

NEXT, the judges dealt with the power exerted by witches. How could the alliance between the Devil and witches exert such power over godly people? How could witches commit the crimes to which they confessed, such as killing a "man, child, horse, cow," or other creature, without God intervening? Didn't it disparage God to believe that He could not prevent the witches under the Devil's command from committing crimes?

Hopkins answered the questions by saying that the God allowed the Devil to do much harm and that the evil the Devil did actually served God's purpose. For his part, the Devil deluded the witches into believing they were committing murders and other crimes. The truth was that the Devil was using the witches as instruments for *his* crimes. The witches were guilty only because they consented to allowing the Devil to use them.

Hopkins reminded the judges that the Devil was fighting a war on earth against God. Hopkins said the earthly war began when the Devil infested the Garden of Eden and tempted Adam and Eve 6,000 years before. The deluding of witches was just one weapon the Devil employed in his ongoing earthly war.

Hopkins continued that the Devil was the "best scholar" in the world. The Devil knew more about arts, languages, and diseases than any man did or ever could. Hopkins held that beyond that, the Devil knew the maladies which each individual human and animal had susceptibility.

Hopkins told the judges that the Devil was a subtle tempter. Knowing that a certain individual was soon to die from a disease such as tuberculosis, the Devil would cause discourse between witches and the dying man.

The Devil would tell the witches that the man had found them out and that he intended to expose them. The Devil said that unless stopped, the man would have the witches searched and would cause the authorities to try them for witchcraft. If that happened, they were certain to swing from the gallows.

Of course, the fear of exposure horrified the witches and they would beg for help.

The Devil would ask the fearful witches. "What will you have me do for you, my dear and nearest children, covenanted and compacted with me in my hellish league, and sealed with your blood, my delicate firebrand-darlings?"

The witches would answer "Oh thou that at the first did promise to save us, thy servants, from any of our deadly enemies' discovery, and did promise to avenge and slay all those, we pleased, that did offend us; murder that wretch suddenly who threatens the downfall of your loyal subjects."

The Devil would promise the witches that he would kill the enemy threatening them. Then, when the man died from the ailment from which he already suffered, the Devil took credit for it. The death of the enemy caused the witches to accord the Devil "a world of reverence, credence and respect."

Hopkins said that a witch increased her "damnation by her familiarity and consent to the Devil" when she honored him for killing an enemy. Additionally, by doing so, she violated human law.

Thus, according to Hopkins, the Devil worked his mischief by deception more than by action. Hopkins said he encouraged the Magistrates and judges to investigate to find out if any of the murders witches confessed to were actually deaths by natural causes.

Hopkins had to contend that the Devil and his witches did commit actual crimes from time to time, however. If witches never committed any crimes, there would be no reason for witch-finders.

The request of the witches for the Devil's help presented above sounded remarkably like a prayer. This dovetails with the Puritan belief that the Devil intended to establish a false religion and to supplant God. Thus, the relationship between the Devil and his witches represented a perverse and reversed mirror image of God's relationship with Christians.

The Puritans backed up what they believed about the Devil's intentions and his relationship with witches by quoting biblical verses. A selection of them follows:

2 Corinthians 4:3-4:

The Puritans believed that the Devil had set himself up as the god of earth and that witches worshipped him as such. 2 Corinthians 4:3-4 seemed to back up that belief:

"But if our gospel be hid, it is hid to them that are lost: In whom the god of this world hath blinded the minds of them which believe not, lest the light of the glorious gospel of Christ, who is the image of God, should shine unto them."

Luke 4:5-6

The Devil was so brazen as to attempt to tempt even Jesus. Although he was unsuccessful, the Devil offered Jesus all the kingdoms of the world. Although Jesus rejected the offer, He did not deny that the Devil could deliver upon his offer. Luke 4:5-6 reads:

"And the devil, taking him up into an high mountain, shewed unto him all the kingdoms of the world in a moment of time. And the devil said unto him, All this power will I give thee, and the glory of them: for that is delivered unto me; and to whomsoever I will I give it."

Ephesians 2:2

Ephesians 2:2 relates that the Devil fostered disobedience to God. Additionally, it asserts that the Devil was the "prince of the power of the air" and that he exerted great power in doing so.

"Wherein in time past ye walked according to the course of this world, according to the prince of the power of the air, the spirit that now worketh in the children of disobedience:"

Ephesians 6:12

The Puritans interpreted Ephesians 6:12 to say that it was their duty to battle against the Devil and his minions.

"For we wrestle not against flesh and blood, but against principalities, against powers, against the rulers of the darkness of this world, against spiritual wickedness in high places."

Isaiah 14:12-14

Isaiah 14:12-14 related that the Devil weakened nations in his attempt to overthrow God's heavenly kingdom and become the master of the universe.

"How art thou fallen from heaven, O Lucifer, son of the morning! how art thou cut down to the ground, which didst weaken the nations! For thou hast said in thine heart, I will ascend into heaven, I will exalt my throne above the stars of God: I will sit also upon the mount of the congregation, in the sides of the north: I will ascend above the heights of the clouds; I will be like the most High."

Revelation 12 3-4, 7-9

Several verses in Revelation speak of the war the Devil waged against God. The verses also comment that the Devil's goal was to deceive the "whole world."

"And there appeared another wonder in heaven; and behold a great red dragon, having seven heads and ten horns, and seven crowns upon his heads. And his tail drew the third part of the stars of heaven, and did cast them to the earth ... And there was war in heaven: Michael and his angels fought against the dragon; and the dragon fought and his angels, And prevailed not; neither was their place found any more in heaven. And the great dragon was cast out, that old serpent, called the Devil, and Satan, which deceiveth the whole world: he was cast out into the earth, and his angels were cast out with him."

15. Was Hopkins a Thief?

BUT if Hopkins was a charlatan and he was purposely accusing innocent people, what were his motives? Those critical of Hopkins claimed that Hopkins fleeced the people of the towns he visited of their money. They said he and his helpers rode into town seeking nothing more than to make money by ferreting out witches. Hopkins assured the townsfolk that many wizards and witches infested the community. He then promised to find the witches and turn them over for hanging – but for a hefty price.

A natural born fear merchant, Hopkins horrified the community with tells of witches ravishing their district, and town fathers paid Hopkins handsomely to find the elusive witches. Yet, Hopkins did nothing for the money he received.

In answering the charges that he was a con artist, Hopkins played the victim. He said he felt wronged by the accusations and he claimed they were all untrue. Then he presented a defense of these charges in three parts:

1. Hopkins said he never went into a town unless someone first rode to him or sent a message for him to come and help. He continued that the people of the towns he visited were happy to have him there.

2. Hopkins said he never accused anyone of being a witch until a search implicated her, or

after she confessed. Hopkins stated that those that observed his actions could testify for him.

3. Hopkins also denied that he fleeced anyone. He said He said that he charged a mere 20 shillings per town and that he rode as many as 20 miles to get to some villages. He said that he remained in each town for as long as a week and that he might find three or four witches wherever he travelled. He contended that even if he found only one witch, twenty shillings was still a good price for his services. The Witch-finder General claimed that he spent everything he earned for the care and feeding of his two helpers, and the three horses he and his men used.

The statements Hopkins made were false. He or one of his agents always went to community and informed the citizens that witches were present there. In the early days of his witch finding, Hopkins had difficulty convincing some community leaders that witchery was afoot. Later, after the witch-mania he engendered raged through the countryside like a forest fire or a deadly virus, Hopkins found it easier to convince the gullible that witches plagued them.

The statement that he never accused anyone of witchcraft until after examiners had performed a search or she had confessed was absurd. The searches and confessions always came *after* Hopkins had made his accusations and the authorities had jailed his victims. Hopkins also applied his various means of torture after he had accused his victims.

Hopkins charged a great deal more than small fees for his services. In those days, the average farm laborer earned about ½ shilling per day. Even if Hopkins stayed in a town for five days, his four shillings a day was eight times what a farm worker made. Besides that, the communities wined and dined Hopkins as if he were a member of nobility while he visited them. They also put up and fed his horses.

Hopkins did not spend very long in any one town and his take averaged much more than four shillings per day. The estimate is that in the period of his witch finding, Hopkins received about £1,000 for his services. It would have taken a field worker more than a century to earn as much money as various towns paid Hopkins in less than three years.

SECTION II: WITCH FINDING TECHNIQUES

THIS section looks at some of the techniques, including tortures, Hopkins and other witch-finders employed.

16. The Bible on Witches

THE Bible spent a lot of time condemning witchcraft. Biblical verses were direct and clear in their intent. They commanded the godly avoid the black arts. If taken literally, as the Puritans did, they allowed witch-finders to commit almost any act against suspects. Thus, the Bible became one of the strongest tools the witch-finders had in their persecution of suspected witches.

Below is a selection from 11 of the 66 books of the Bible dealing with witchcraft.

Exodus 22:18:

The most famous anti-witch biblical verse is Exodus 22:18. The verse, taken literally, commands the execution of anyone proven guilty of witchcraft.

"Thou shalt not suffer a witch to live."

Leviticus 19:31:

Leviticus 19:31 was not as strong in condemning witches as was the previous verse was. It did not mandate the execution of witches directly. It merely demanded that the godly ignore and ostracize witches. On the other hand, the verse did nothing to mitigate the idea that witchcraft was a capital offense.

As we shall see, the next chapter of Leviticus reaffirmed that witchcraft was a capital offense.

"Regard not them that have familiar spirits, neither seek after wizards, to be defiled by them: I am the Lord your God."

Leviticus 20:6:

Leviticus 20:6 warned that God intended to punish those that followed the ways of witches by ostracizing them.

"And the soul that turneth after such as have familiar spirits, and after wizards, to go a whoring after them, I will even set my face against that soul, and will cut him off from among his people."

Leviticus 20:27:

Leviticus got around to condemning witches to death in verse 20:27. The verse confirmed that both men and women could be witches and it mandated the exact same penalty for them regardless of gender. It ordered that witches suffer death by stoning.

"A man also or woman that hath a familiar spirit, or that is a wizard, shall surely be put to death: they shall stone them with stones: their blood shall be upon them."

Deuteronomy 18:9-14:

Deuteronomy 18:9-14 cautioned against the "abominations" associated with witchcraft. Some of the abominations mentioned included fortunetelling, consorting with familiar spirits and necromancy (communicating with, or reanimating the dead).

"When thou art come into the land which the Lord thy God giveth thee, thou shalt not learn to do after the abominations of those nations. There shall not be found among you any one that maketh his son or his daughter to pass through the fire, or that useth divination, or an observer of times, or an enchanter, or a witch. Or a charmer, or a consulter with familiar spirits, or a wizard, or a necromancer. For all that do these things are an abomination unto the Lord: and because of these abominations the Lord thy God doth drive them out from before thee. Thou shalt be perfect with the Lord thy God. For these nations, which thou shalt possess, hearkened unto observers of times, and unto diviners: but as for thee, the Lord thy God hath not suffered thee so to do."

1 Samuel 15:23:

1 Samuel 15:23 compared military rebellion to witchcraft. This implies that witches were soldiers in the Devil's Army of rebellion against God.

"For rebellion is as the sin of witchcraft, and stubbornness is as iniquity and idolatry. Because thou hast rejected the word of the Lord, he hath also rejected thee from being king."

1 Samuel 28:3-25:

One of the most famous stories in the Bible relating to witchcraft is found in 1 Samuel 28:3-25. It states that although King Saul had punished witches with death, he himself sinned when he enlisted the aid of the Witch of Endore. He asked the soothsayer to raise the spirit of Samuel, so that Saul could get advice from the dead prophet.

"Now Samuel was dead, and all Israel had lamented him, and buried him in Ramah, even in his own city. And Saul had put away those that had familiar spirits, and the wizards, out of the land. And the Philistines gathered themselves together, and came and pitched in Shunem: and Saul gathered all Israel together, and they pitched in Gilboa. And when Saul saw the host of the Philistines, he was afraid, and his heart greatly trembled. And when Saul enquired of the Lord, the Lord answered him not, neither by dreams, nor by Urim, nor by prophets. Then said Saul unto his servants, Seek me a woman that hath a familiar spirit, that I may go to her, and enquire of her. And his servants said to him, Behold, there is a woman that hath a familiar spirit at Endor. And Saul disguised himself, and put on other raiment, and he went, and two men with him, and they came to the woman by night: and he said, I pray thee, divine unto me by the familiar spirit, and bring me him up, whom I shall name unto thee. And the woman said unto him, Behold, thou knowest what Saul hath done, how he hath cut off those that have familiar spirits, and the wizards, out of the land:

wherefore then layest thou a snare for my life, to cause me to die? And Saul sware to her by the Lord, saying, As the Lord liveth, there shall no punishment happen to thee for this thing. Then said the woman, Whom shall I bring up unto thee? And he said, Bring me up Samuel. And when the woman saw Samuel, she cried with a loud voice: and the woman spake to Saul, saying, Why hast thou deceived me? for thou art Saul. And the king said unto her, Be not afraid: for what sawest thou? And the woman said unto Saul, I saw gods ascending out of the earth. And he said unto her, What form is he of? And she said, An old man cometh up; and he is covered with a mantle. And Saul perceived that it was Samuel, and he stooped with his face to the ground, and bowed himself. And Samuel said to Saul, Why hast thou disquieted me, to bring me up? And Saul answered, I am sore distressed; for the Philistines make war against me, and God is departed from me, and answereth me no more, neither by prophets, nor by dreams: therefore I have called thee, that thou mayest make known unto me what I shall do. Then said Samuel, Wherefore then dost thou ask of me, seeing the Lord is departed from thee, and is become thine enemy? And the Lord hath done to him, as he spake by me: for the Lord hath rent the kingdom out of thine hand, and given it to thy neighbour, even to David: Because thou obeyedst not the voice of the Lord, nor executedst his fierce wrath upon Amalek, therefore hath the Lord done this thing unto thee this day. Moreover the Lord will also deliver Israel with thee into the hand of the

Philistines: and to morrow shalt thou and thy sons be with me: the Lord also shall deliver the host of Israel into the hand of the Philistines. Then Saul fell straightway all along on the earth, and was sore afraid, because of the words of Samuel: and there was no strength in him; for he had eaten no bread all the day, nor all the night. And the woman came unto Saul, and saw that he was sore troubled, and said unto him, Behold, thine handmaid hath obeyed thy voice, and I have put my life in my hand, and have hearkened unto thy words which thou spakest unto me. Now therefore, I pray thee, hearken thou also unto the voice of thine handmaid, and let me set a morsel of bread before thee; and eat, that thou mayest have strength, when thou goest on thy way. But he refused, and said, I will not eat. But his servants, together with the woman, compelled him; and he hearkened unto their voice. So he arose from the earth, and sat upon the bed. And the woman had a fat calf in the house; and she hasted, and killed it, and took flour, and kneaded it, and did bake unleavened bread thereof: And she brought it before Saul, and before his servants; and they did eat. Then they rose up, and went away that night.

1 Chronicles 10:13:

1 Chronicles 10:13 relates that King Saul died because he committed transgressions against the Lord. Among Saul's transgressions was enlisting the aid of the Witch of Endore.

"So Saul died for his transgression which he committed against the Lord, even against the word of the Lord, which he kept not, and also for asking counsel of one that had a familiar spirit, to enquire of it."

2 Chronicles 33:6:

2 Chronicles 33:6 is another verse stating that dealing with witches was evil and that it angered God.

"And he caused his children to pass through the fire in the valley of the son of Hinnom: also he observed times, and used enchantments, and used witchcraft, and dealt with a familiar spirit, and with wizards: he wrought much evil in the sight of the Lord, to provoke him to anger."

Isaiah 8:19-22:

Isaiah 8:19-22 encouraged people to seek God and avoid witches. Otherwise, they would live in darkness.

"And when they shall say unto you, Seek unto them that have familiar spirits, and unto wizards that peep, and that mutter: should not a people seek unto their God? for the living to the dead? To the law and to the testimony: if they speak not according to this word, it is because there is no light in them. And they shall pass through it, hardly bestead and hungry: and it shall come to pass, that when they shall be hungry, they shall fret themselves, and curse their king and their God, and look upward. And they shall look unto the earth;

and behold trouble and darkness, dimness of anguish; and they shall be driven to darkness."

Isaiah 19:1-4:

Isaiah 19:1-4 condemned Egypt to destruction for, among other things, allowing the practice of witchcraft.

"The burden of Egypt. Behold, the Lord rideth upon a swift cloud, and shall come into Egypt: and the idols of Egypt shall be moved at his presence, and the heart of Egypt shall melt in the midst of it. And I will set the Egyptians against the Egyptians: and they shall fight every one against his brother, and every one against his neighbour; city against city, and kingdom against kingdom. And the spirit of Egypt shall fail in the midst thereof; and I will destroy the counsel thereof: and they shall seek to the idols, and to the charmers, and to them that have familiar spirits, and to the wizards. And the Egyptians will I give over into the hand of a cruel lord; and a fierce king shall rule over them, saith the Lord, the Lord of hosts."

Isaiah 47:8-14:

Isaiah 47:8-14 cautioned people not to partake of idle pleasures such as fortunetelling and witchcraft.

"Therefore hear now this, thou that art given to pleasures, that dwellest carelessly, that sayest in thine heart, I am, and none else beside me; I shall not sit as a widow, neither shall I know the loss of children: But these two things shall come to thee in a moment in one day, the loss of children, and widowhood: they shall come upon thee in their perfection for the multitude of thy sorceries, and for the great abundance of thine enchantments. For thou hast trusted in thy wickedness: thou hast said, None seeth me. Thy wisdom and thy knowledge, it hath perverted thee; and thou hast said in thine heart, I am, and none else beside me. Therefore shall evil come upon thee; thou shalt not know from whence it riseth: and mischief shall fall upon thee; thou shalt not be able to put it off: and desolation shall come upon thee suddenly, which thou shalt not know. Stand now with thine enchantments, and with the multitude of thy sorceries, wherein thou hast laboured from thy youth; if so be thou shalt be able to profit, if so be thou mayest prevail. Thou art wearied in the multitude of thy counsels. Let now the astrologers, the stargazers, the monthly prognosticators, stand up, and save thee from these things that shall come upon thee. Behold, they shall be as stubble; the fire shall burn them; they shall not deliver themselves from the power of the flame: there shall not be a coal to warm at, nor fire to sit before it."

Micah 5:10-12:

Micah 5:10-12 promised to punish sinful people and their witches.

"And it shall come to pass in that day, saith the Lord, that I will cut off thy horses out of the midst of thee, and I will destroy thy chariots: And I will cut off the cities of thy land, and throw down all thy strong holds: And I will cut off witchcrafts out of thine hand; and thou shalt have no more soothsayers:"

Acts 8:9-13:

Acts 8: 9-13 relates one of the more famous Bible stories. It deals with a man from Samaria named Simon. This Simon (considered by many biblical scholars to be the Gnostic leader, Simon Magus) bewitched people of his region through sorcery and became very powerful.

"But there was a certain man, called Simon, which beforetime in the same city used sorcery, and bewitched the people of Samaria, giving out that himself was some great one: To whom they all gave heed, from the least to the greatest, saying, This man is the great power of God. And to him they had regard, because that of long time he had bewitched them with sorceries. But when they believed Philip preaching the things concerning the kingdom of God, and the name of Jesus Christ, they were baptized, both men and women. Then Simon himself believed also: and when he was baptized, he continued with Philip, and wondered, beholding the miracles and signs which were done.

Acts 8:18-23:

Then Acts 18-23 related that the charlatan Simon lacked the power of healing displayed by the Apostles of God. In an attempt to gain that power, Simon offered to purchase it from the

Disciples of Christ. The Apostle Peter refused the sorcerer and sent him away.

"And when Simon saw that through laying on of the apostles' hands the Holy Ghost was given, he offered them money, Saying, Give me also this power, that on whomsoever I lay hands, he may receive the Holy Ghost. But Peter said unto him, Thy money perish with thee, because thou hast thought that the gift of God may be purchased with money. Thou hast neither part nor lot in this matter: for thy heart is not right in the sight of God. Repent therefore of this thy wickedness, and pray God, if perhaps the thought of thine heart may be forgiven thee. For I perceive that thou art in the gall of bitterness, and in the bond of iniquity."

Acts 19: 17-20:

Acts 19: 17-20 relates that it was possible for witches to reform. The passage stated that at Ephesus many of the sorcerers abandoned their "curious arts," burned their books on witchcraft, and became faithful Christians. The Puritans too, believed that witches could reform. Puritans seldom executed witches that displayed remorse and confessed.

"And this was known to all the Jews and Greeks also dwelling at Ephesus; and fear fell on them all, and the name of the Lord Jesus was magnified. And many that believed came, and confessed, and shewed their deeds. Many of them also which used curious arts brought their books together, and burned them before all men: and they counted the price of them, and found it fifty thousand pieces of silver. So mightily grew the word of God and prevailed."

Galatians 5:19-21:

Galatians 5:19-21 listed witchcraft as a work of the flesh and stated that those that practiced it would not get to Heaven.

"Now the works of the flesh are manifest, which are these; Adultery, fornication, uncleanness, lasciviousness, Idolatry, witchcraft, hatred, variance, emulations, wrath, strife, seditions, heresies, Envyings, murders, drunkenness, revellings, and such like: of the which I tell you before, as I have also told you in time past, that they which do such things shall not inherit the kingdom of God."

Revelation 18:23:

Revelation 18:23 condemns those nations that turned away from God and deceived others with their sorceries.

"And the light of a candle shall shine no more at all in thee; and the voice of the bridegroom and of the bride shall be heard no more at all in thee: for thy merchants were the great men of the earth; for by thy sorceries were all nations deceived."

Revelation 21:8:

Revelation 21:8 gives a list of those certain to burn in Hellfire. The list included sorcerers.

"But the fearful, and unbelieving, and the abominable, and murderers, and whoremongers, and sorcerers, and idolaters, and all liars, shall have their part in the lake which burneth with fire and brimstone: which is the second death."

Believing that the Bible commanded them to suppress witchcraft and persecute witches, ardent Puritans such as Matthew Hopkins felt justified in taking brutal and extreme measures to locate and dispose of witches.

17. The Devil's Book

PURITANS put a great deal of stock in the Devil's Book. They believed that a witch confirmed her covenants with the Devil by signing the book he carried for such purposes. The book supposedly held all the names of all of the Devil's witches.

The idea was that if one had the book, he could quickly identify all the witches in a given area. Of course, the book was of such grave importance, that the only way to get it would have been with the Devil's consent. Thus, the judges concluded that if Matthew Hopkins had the book, it proved he was a witch. Of course, he denied that he ever saw the Devil's Book and no one attempted to find it on his person.

What resulted when one signed the Devil's Book?" The Puritans believed that when a witch signed her name, or made her mark in the book, "with pen and ink" or in her own blood, it made her contract with the Devil binding for eternity. After she signed the book, so they thought, the Devil granted the witch the supernatural powers he had promised to her. These powers sometimes included the ability to fly, to move around in the form of a spirit, to have familiars or imps at her disposal, to harm others through magical acts, or even to control the weather.

The belief in the Devil's Book was an important part of witch trials and witch courts put great stock in proving that the accused signed it. For instance, at Salem accusers routinely testified that they saw the names of the accused in the Devil's Book and if a witch confessed to signing the book, it clinched her conviction.

For some of the accused at Salem, the only testimony against them was that they tried or succeeded in persuading a person to sign the Devil's Book. That testimony alone was especially damming, because it implied that the witch was actively recruiting witches for the Devil's Army.

Origins of the Belief

The idea of the Devil's Book may have derived from the Puritan belief that that church members made a pact with God when they signed the church membership book.

The Puritans believed the Devil was attempting to overthrow God's religion and replace it with his own, and it made sense to them that those joining the Devil's cult would sign a membership book. Thus, church leaders contended that signing the Devil's Book directly undermined local church authority. Samuel Parris and other Puritan preachers in Salem hammered away at the idea that rooting out witches made the local church stronger.

The Puritans may also have believed that they had a biblical foundation for their belief in the Devil's Book. The Bible never mentions the Devil's book, but it does mention its counterpart. New Testament writers related the existence of a Book of Life that existed in Heaven.

Luke 10:20 "Notwithstanding in this rejoice not, that the spirits are subject unto you; but rather rejoice, because your names are written in heaven."

Philippians 4:3: "And I intreat thee also, true yokefellow, help those women which laboured with me in the gospel, with Clement also, and with other my fellow labourers, whose names are in the book of life."

Again, the Puritans believed that the Devil was attempting to build a religion that perverted Christianity, thus it would follow that if God had the names of the godly in the Book of Life, then the Devil would have the names of his followers in a book as well.

Tituba and the Devil's Book

Samuel Parris held a woman named Tituba in slavery. Called before Judge John Hathorne, she confirmed what the Puritans already believed about the Devil's Book. However, it appears that she was merely repeating what the judge wanted to hear.

Tituba confessed to signing the Devil's Book, as well as to doing other things that "proved" she was a witch. She did not volunteer that she signed the book up front, but only said so during withering questioning from Judge Hathorne. When he asked her if she signed the book, she said she did "with red like blood."

When asked if she had seen other "marks" in the Devil's Book when she signed it, Tituba said she had. She claimed to see the marks made by Sarah Good and Sarah Osborne as well as the names or marks of seven other witches. Tituba said she couldn't remember the names of the seven other witches.

In England during the days of Matthew Hopkins, authorities sometimes executed confessed witches. In Massachusetts, they never executed confessed witches. Because she had confessed and implicated others, Tituba avoided the gallows.

Based partially on Tituba's testimony that they had signed the Devil's Book, Osborne and Good suffered death. Sarah Osborne died in jail on May 10, 1692, and the authorities executed Sarah Good on July 29, 1692.

Other accusers at Salem gave specifics about signing the Devil's Book. The testimony usually included allegations that the accused came to their victims as specters (spirits) and had tried to force them to sign the book. The accusers claimed that when they refused to sign the Devil's Book, the witches made them promises of wealth and happiness. When that failed, the witches made threats and even tortured the accusers to a point near death. The accusers took a heroic stance. They said that despite the torture they experienced, they didn't sign, or even touch the Devil's Book.

Specific testimony about the Devil's Book came from Abigail Williams. In March 1692, she gave a deposition claiming that Rebecca

Nurse had tried to force her to sign the Devil's Book. Authorities executed Rebecca Nurse on July 19, 1692.

In April 1692, Mercy Lewis testified that Giles Corey appeared before her in the form of a spirit and forced her to sign the Devil's Book. Four days later, authorities arrested Giles Corey and charged him with witchcraft. As related earlier, Corey refused to confirm or deny the charges against him and the court ordered him pressed by stones. Corey died from his ordeal on September 19, 1692.

History of the Belief

While the Puritans were strong believers in the Devil's Book, the belief did not originate with them. More than two centuries before the Salem witch trials, a German monk wrote *Malleus Maleficarum.* Written in Latin, *Malleus Maleficarum* became one of the most common manuals employed by witch-finders in Europe. The book contended that the oral or written agreement with the Devil was a critical ritual in the initiation of a witch into the Devil's cult.

18. Witch Hunting Guides

IF witch-hunters had a mind to, they could rely on a few manuals to help them. One was *Daemonologie* (Demonology) by King James. James was an important person in English history. Not only did he become king of the British Empire, but he also authorized a translation of the Bible into English. This version of the Bible, which bears his name, was the standard religious scripture used by Protestant Christians in the English-speaking world for centuries. Many Christians continue to use it to this day.

James, then King of Scotland, published *Daemonologie* in 1597 and it covered many topics concerning black magic and witchery. James had the book reissued in 1603 when he ascended to the throne of England.

Daemonologie was both political and theological in scope. It was a study in how James believed that witches chastised troubled men. It was also a textbook intended to teach an uninformed populace about the history, practices, and implications of witchcraft. James intended *Daemonologie* to provide justification for the persecution and execution of the witches infiltrating his realm.

James wrote *Daemonologie* in three books and in a style of a Socratic dialogue. *Daemonologie* condemned all forms of magic, sorcery, and witchcraft. James even grouped various demons into classes.

King James had personal acquaintance with witch trials. Beginning in 1590, he was involved in the North Berwick witch trials, and those trials influenced his ideas about sorcery. James included a pamphlet called *Newes from Scotland* at the end of *Daemonologie*. The pamphlet detailed some of the North Berwick witch trials.

James endorsed hunting witches. He contented that the "detestable slaves of the Devil" abounded in Scotland and elsewhere. He stated that he intended to "resolve the doubting" that the Devil employed witches to assault the godly. He also intended to prove that witches deserved severe punishment.

James assured his readers that he was not simply stating his own opinions, but that he based his thesis on historic confessions of witches, previous witch trials, and the Bible. He also referenced a large body of works on the study of magic. This, he thought gave him insight into the relationship between evil spirits and humans.

James conceded that the Devil had always sought to corrupt humans and to drive a wedge between them and God. He repeated that those that gave themselves over to the Devil deserved punishment. He acknowledged that many Christians who were not under the influence of the Devil still doubted that witches were committing crimes or that they even existed. To counter this, James relied on Biblical teaching to prove his theory.

Book One

The first part of *Daemonologie* covered the following topics:

1. A discussion of the various black arts with a comparison of witchcraft and Necromancy.

2. The use of charms, circles, and conjuring.

3. Astrology.

4. The Devil's contracts with witches.

5. Comparisons between the miracles of God and the magic of the Devil.

6. The first part ends with the assertion that God allows the Devil and his minions to work their mischief in an attempt to advise the people as to the difference between good and evil.

Book Two

Book Two dealt with the following topics dealing with witchcraft:

1. The difference between biblical proof and conjecture or myth.

2. A comparison of sorcery and witchcraft.

3. The activities of a sorcerer's apprentice.

4. Curses and the roles adopted by the Devil.

5. The times demons appear and the forms they take.

6. Comparisons of the actions taken by witches.

7. The second part ends with a discussion of the methods transportation and the illusions of the Devil.

Book Three

The third book concludes the monologue and ties its various elements together. King James asserts that demons are under the ultimate control of God and that they cannot act without His permission. James also contends that uses the demonic forces as a "Rod of Correction" when men become too sinful. James continued that witches and magicians could also enlist demons to commit acts of ill will against their enemies.

James quoted other authors on the subject. Then he detailed the ability of demons to change shape to fit the purpose at hand. James also attempted to prove that despite the attempts of demons to aid the Devil, in the end, their actions led to the greater glorification of God.

James then classified the various kinds of demons that plagued the world. He did not sort the demons by their names, ranks, or titles. Instead, he collected them together according to the methods they used to obtain their devilish ends. The four classifications of demons identified by James were:

1. Spectra: The Spectra, in the mind of James, were identical, or very similar to, the *Lemures* of Roman mythology. The Romans believed the *Lemures* were wandering and vengeful spirits of those that did not receive proper burial or funeral rites.

James said these spirits ordinarily haunted "solitary places," but that the Devil could cause them to take "terrible forms" and haunt the houses of those weak in God's spirit. James held that God allowed the Spectra to haunt houses as a form punishment. Only those that displayed a "gross ignorance" of God's will, or had committed "some gross and slanderous" act against God, experienced visits from the Spectra.

2. Obsession: James called another class of demons, "Obsession." This class of demons was similar to incubi, succubae, and even to the vampires. Belief in these demons was ancient and James covered old ground when he wrote about them. However, James described the actions of these demons a bit differently than earlier writers had.

According to James, demons of the Obsession class could impregnate women. The impregnation could happen in one of two ways. The first method a demon could use was to steal the sperm from a dead man and then insert it into a woman. The second method involved the demon possessing a corpse, causing it to rise and then using it to have sexual relations with a woman.

3. Possession: King James believed, as did the Roman Catholic Church, that demons could possess humans. He also agreed that one could discern demonic possession from natural diseases. However, he disagreed with the

Roman Catholics as to the signs of possession and the means to drive out demons. James denied that holy water would be burn a possessed person or that the possessed feared the cross. James held the Catholic rites of exorcism were counterfeit because they cured few if any possessed people.

James ascribed to the method of casting out demons mentioned in the Bible. He wrote, "It is easy then to understand that the casting out of Devils is by the virtue of fasting and prayer, and in calling of the name of God."

4. Fairies: James listed the fourth class of demon as "Faries." The fairies that James believed in were not the benign, cute little spirits as portrayed in so many movies, cartoons, and television shows. He saw fairies as demonic spirits that prophesied to, consorted with, and transported the witches they served.

The familiar spirits that fed off the blood of witches, and aided them in murders and other crimes fell into the category of fairies. James held that locating evidence that a witch had a familiar spirit was enough to send her to the gallows.

Newes from Scotland

The final chapter of *Daemonologie* consisted of a pamphlet called *Newes From Scotland* originally published in 1591. *Newes From Scotland* detailed accounts of the North Berwick witch trials. King James acted as the judge during some of those trials. About 150 persons suffered arrest and many confessed after being tortured during the Scottish witch mania. The authorities eventually hung 25 people convicted of witchcraft during the trials.

The Hammer of Sorceresses

Another textbook used by witch-finders bore the title *Malleus Maleficarum.* Usually translated "Hammer of Witches," or "Hammer of Sorceresses," *Malleus Maleficarum* is the best-known book encouraging the tracking down and killing of witches. Working under the penname "Henricus Institor," a German monk named Heinrich Kramer published *Malleus Maleficarum* in the German city of Speyer in 1486. The book proved to be the definitive source of means to persecute witches.

Malleus Maleficarum did not receive universal acceptance early on. The administrators of the Inquisition at the Faculty of Cologne condemned the book because it encouraged methods that were illegal and unethical. They also asserted that *Malleus Maleficarum* was in variance with many accepted Roman Catholic doctrines concerning demonology.

Malleus Maleficarum stated that witchcraft was criminal heresy and recommended that secular courts prosecute it as a capital offense. The book favored torture as the most effective means of gaining confessions and proclaimed that the only effective means of countering witches was by executing them.

Royal Courts and witch-hunters for the next several centuries cited *Malleus Maleficarum* as a source in justifying the persecuting sorcerers.

Malleus Maleficarum became the handbook for judges of secular courts throughout Europe. However, leaders of the Inquisition apparently did not consult it often.

Heinrich Kramer explained that he wrote *Malleus Maleficarum* because of the prevalence of witchcraft in the world. He also informed his readers that Lucifer was making his final assault on God's realm and that he was using witches to help him.

Kramer stated that the Devil was mounting his final assault at that particular time and was causing evil of men to "swell up" because that "he has little time remaining. Hence, he has also caused a certain unusual heretical perversity to grow up in the land of the Lord."

Kramer also made an important assertion that affected future witch-hunts. Kramer wrote that the Devil had greater power over women than he did over men.

Papal Bull

Malleus Maleficarum included a public decree issued by Pope Innocent VIII. Such decrees, known as Papal Bulls carried the weight of law in those times. This Papal Bull, called *Summis Desiderantes Affectibus* (*Desiring with supreme ardor*), acknowledged that witches were real and that they harmed society by doing the will of the Devil. Although the Pope issued the decree on December 5,

1484 (two years before the publication of *Malleus Maleficarum*), it appeared to validate the views expressed in the book. The Papal Bull read in part:

"Many persons of both sexes, unmindful of their own salvation and straying from the Catholic Faith, have abandoned themselves to devils, incubi and succubi, and by their incantations, spells, conjurations, and other accursed charms and crafts, enormities and horrid offences, have slain infants yet in the mother's womb, as also the offspring of cattle, have blasted the produce of the earth, the grapes of the vine, the fruits of the trees, nay, men and women, beasts of burthen, herd-beasts, as well as animals of other kinds, vineyards, orchards, meadows, pasture-land, corn, wheat, and all other cereals; these wretches furthermore afflict and torment men and women, beasts of burthen, herd-beasts, as well as animals of other kinds, with terrible and piteous pains and sore diseases, both internal and external; they hinder men from performing the sexual act and women from conceiving ... they blIhemously renounce that Faith which is theirs by the Sacrament of Baptism, and at the instigation of the Enemy of Mankind they do not shrink from committing and perpetrating the foulest abominations and filthiest excesses to the deadly peril of their own souls ... the abominations and enormities in question remain unpunished not without open danger to the souls of many and peril of eternal damnation."

Malleus Maleficarum stated the opinion that that there were three elements necessary for witchcraft:

1. The evil intentions of the witch.

2. The help of the Devil.

3. The permission of God.

The book contends that witchcraft is not imaginary or a product of "deluding phantasms of the devil," nor is it "simply the fantasies of overwrought human minds." On the contrary, *Malleus Maleficarum* declares that witchcraft must be real, because the Devil is real. Witches were witches because they entered into eternal contracts with the Devil and he helped them perform their wickedness.

Malleus Maleficarum continued that witches, not the Devil, did most of the recruiting of new witches into the evil band. They did this, according to the book, by causing mishaps in the lives of respectable people – especially women. The misfortune caused the otherwise good women to turn to the witch for help and she convinced them to give themselves to the Devil.

Malleus Maleficarum described another way witches brought others into the Devil's orbit. Witches would introduce young, unmarried women and little girls to demons that would tempt them. Thus, *Malleus Maleficarum* introduced a strange sexual component into the recruitment of witches. Apparently, Kramer thought that naïve females made easy prey for the Devil.

How to Prosecute Witches

Malleus Maleficarum contained a long section describing the how to prosecute witches. The systematic guide included:

1. The method of initiating a witch-hunt.

2. Accumulating accusations.

3. The interrogation of witches – this included physical torture.

4. Finally, the book included the method of charging of persons with practicing witchcraft formally.

According to *Malleus Maleficarum*, if an accused witch did not cry during her trial, she was certainly guilty. Matthew Hopkins stated his belief in this idea too.

Malleus Maleficarum not only condoned torture it encouraged it. Beyond that, the book encouraged interrogators to deceive the accused:

"And when the implements of torture have been prepared, the judge, both in person and through other good men zealous in the faith, tries to persuade the prisoner to confess the truth freely; but, if he will not confess, he bid attendants make the prisoner fast to the strappado or some other implement of torture. The attendants obey forthwith, yet with feigned agitation. Then, at the prayer of some of those present, the prisoner is loosed again and is taken aside and once more persuaded to confess, being led to believe that he will in that case not be put to death."

A strappado (also known as a corda or "reverse hanging") was a form of torture in which witch-finders tied the victim's wrists behind his back, and suspended the victim by his wrists. Sometimes, the torturers added weight to the victim's lower body to increase the pain. The bouts of torture by means of strappado often resulted in the separated shoulders, or even death. During the Vietnam War, North Vietnam authorities tortured American soldiers by use of simple strappado devices.

Malleus Maleficarum mandated that suspects confirm all confessions they made under torture.

"And note that, if he confesses under the torture, he must afterward be conducted to another place, that he may confirm it and certify that it was not due alone to the force of the torture. But, if the prisoner will not confess the truth satisfactorily, other sorts of tortures must be placed before him, with the statement that unless he will confess the truth, he must endure these also. But, if not even thus he can be brought into terror and to the truth, then the next day or the next but one is to be set for a continuation of the tortures – not a repetition, for it must not be repeated unless new evidences produced. The judge must then address to the prisoners the following sentence: We, the judge, etc., do assign to you, such and such a day for the continuation of the tortures, that from your own mouth the truth may be heard, and that the whole may be recorded by the notary."

Of course, requiring confirmation meant nothing. If the victim did not repeat the confession, the interrogators applied new and more insidious tortures.

Victims

Malleus Maleficarum related a theory as to how men and women came to practice witchcraft. The book put forth the idea that women were more likely to become witches because they were weaker in faith and more carnal in nature than were men. This belief may help to explain why about three-quarters of those Matthews Hopkins accused of witchcraft were women.

19. Witch Sabbaths

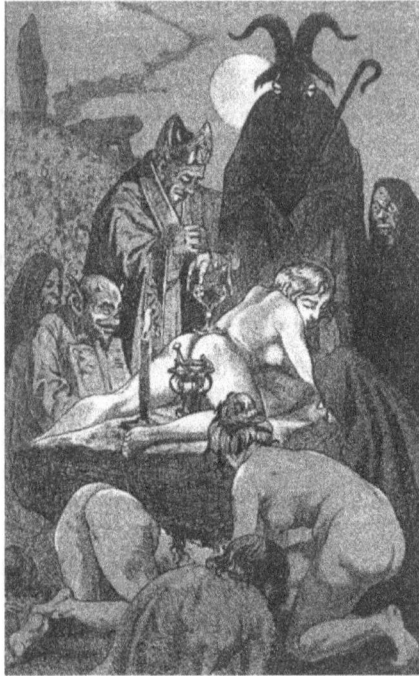

WITCH-FINDERS spent a great deal of time discussing assemblies they called "Witch Sabbaths". A brief look at Witch Sabbaths follows below.

Supposed Witch Sabbaths (aka Witch Synagogues) were nighttime gatherings attended by large numbers of the Devil's servants and sometimes, but not always, by the Devil himself. Written acknowledgement of Witch Sabbaths in Christian Europe date from around 1350 A.D. when mention of them first appeared in the records of the Inquisition. However, the belief in Witch Sabbaths is much older than that. In pre-Christian Rome, noted authors including Petronius Arbiter and Lucius Apuleius wrote of revelries and feasts that resembled the Witch Sabbaths described in later times.

The Christians called assemblies of witches Sabbaths because of the supposed religious significance the participants ascribed to the meetings. However, according to the belief, most Witch Sabbaths took place on Fridays, instead the traditional Sabbath Day (Saturday for Jewish people, and Sunday for most Christians).

The reported attendance of Witch Sabbaths varied, often by the population of the location of the alleged assembly. They were usually described has having 100 or so witches present, but in Europe, one confessed witch said she attended a Sabbath with 10,000 other witches.

Witches confessed that they flew through the air to meetings on poles or brooms. They gained the ability to fly by applying "flying ointment" either to their bodies or to their vehicles. Sometimes the witches flew alone, other times they rode in tandem with other witches on the same broom. Not all witches said they flew to Sabbaths. Some claimed they rode on goats, sheep, or dogs that the Devil provided to them.

Alleged Witch Sabbaths took place in many, many places in both Europe and America. Some of the more famous locales of supposed Witch Sabbaths included:

1. Brocken, Germany.

2. Kiev, Russia.

3. Blockula (Blåkulla), Sweden.

4. Auvergne, France.

5. Auld Kirk Green, Scotland.

6. Manningtree, England.

7. Salem Village, Massachusetts.

Matthew Hopkins stated that he observed witches holding Sabbaths every six weeks. This would mean that they held eight or nine assemblies yearly.

This mostly agreed with the idea shared by most witch-finders that witches attended eight large festivals every year.

The names and dates of those Witch Festivals were:

1. Imbolc: Celebrated on February 2, also known as Oimelc and Candlemas.

2. Ostara: Celebrated on March 21 or about the time of the Spring Equinox.

3. Beltane: Celebrated on April 30, also known as Roodmas, May Day Eve, and Walpurgis Night.

4. Litha: Celebrated on June 21 or about the time of the Summer Solstice.

5. Lughnasadh: Celebrated on August 1., also known as Lammas.

6. Mabon: Celebrated on September 21, or about the time of the Autumn Equinox.

7. Halloween: October 31. Also known as All Hallows Eve, Hallowmas, and Samhain.

8. Yule: Celebrated on December 21 or about the time of the Winter Solstice.

Some of the activities associated with Witch Sabbaths included:

1. Praising the Devil.

2. Signing the Devil's Book.

3. Nude dancing.

4. Unrestrained sexual intercourse and orgies.

5. Feasting on stolen meat, produce, and wine.

6. Kissing the Devil "under his tail."

7. Planning the overthrow of God's Kingdom.

8. Sacrificing animals and humans.

20. Familiar Spirits and Imps

WITCH-FINDERS believed that witches received aid in their evil ways from familiar spirits (often called imps). These supernatural beings, created by the Devil, could take on many forms. They usually came as animals, or grotesque creatures, but sometimes as humans as well. Although they were spirits, familiars were not shadowy or translucent as Puritans believed ghosts to be. Familiar spirits were clearly defined, three-dimensional creatures. Often brightly colored, they moved easily, made sounds, and could speak to their witches and other humans.

Being of the Devil, familiar spirits shared his malevolence. The main purpose of familiar spirits was to fulfill the designs of the Devil by aiding witches in their crimes.

Some of the witches that described their familiar spirits related that they were strange looking, even monstrous in appearance. Others stated that they were ordinary looking, and represented common creatures. Most often, familiar spirits had the shapes of small animals, such as cats, rats, dogs, ferrets, birds, frogs, toads, hares, and turtles. There were also cases of witches describing familiars as having the shapes of wasps, butterflies, pigs, sheep, and horses.

As stated in Chapter 6, familiar spirits had names that identified them. Some of the names were common, and others that were strange.

Familiars and Witch Trials

Most of the information we have about familiar spirits comes from confessions obtained at various witch trials. Since the inquisitors had preconceived notions as to what familiars were like and what they did, the descriptions of them have a certain consistency. In most cases, the familiar spirits took on roles as intermediaries between witches and the Devil. Occasionally, witches appeared to have affection for their familiars and thought of them as surrogate children.

The Massachusetts law of 1648 defined a witch as one who "hath or consulteth with a familiar spirit." Although colonial authorities suspended the law a decade before the Salem witch trials, the idea that witches consulted with familiar spirits still weighed on the minds of the judges. The judges accepted claims that individuals employed familiar spirits as proof positive of witchcraft.

During the Salem witch-hunts, accusers often claimed to see the familiars in the company of witches. Some of the accusers even claimed to observe familiars feeding off the blood of witches. Anne Putnam testified that she saw a familiar spirit in the shape of a yellow bird draw blood from a witch's teat between two of Martha Corey's fingers. In open court, Putnam said to Corey, "There is a yellow bird a sucking between your forefinger and middle finger. I see it."

The slave woman Tituba testified that "strange" animals urged her to harm children.

The animals that spoke to Tituba included a hog, a black dog, a red cat, and a black cat.

Prince Rupert's Dog

Over time, several ordinary animals earned the reputation of being familiar spirits, or if not familiar spirits per se, having demonic powers.

One of the most well known alleged familiar spirits was a dog that followed his host into combat. During the English Civil War, Royalist General Prince Rupert of the Rhine brought his large poodle named "Boy" into combat with him.

Boy was not the sweet pretty, little, pink dog most of us imagine when we think of poodles. He was a fierce beast. The vicious canine ripped up many of Cromwell's soldiers and they feared meeting him on the battlefield. The legend of the ferocious dog grew and myth arose that Boy had supernatural powers – that he was a familiar spirit.

Boy followed Rupert into combat at the Battle of Marston Moor on July 2, 1644. During the conflict a soldier of Cromwell's Army shot and killed Boy, allegedly with a silver bullet.

The truth is that the legend of the familiar spirit Boy was more propaganda than reality. The dog was a formidable fighter, but no more so than many other dogs. Besides that, no one ever accused Rupert of being a witch.

During the Salem witch mania, courts accepted as a fact that ordinary dogs could be demented. Authorities charged a man with using magic to compel a dog to attack people. Witch-finders captured the dog (but not the man), the court convicted it of witchcraft, and the Sheriff hanged it.

21. Witch Cakes

DOGS played one other major role at Salem. They had the task of proving that the girls showing the first signs of affliction were victims of witchery.

When the girls in the household of preacher Samuel Parris began to have "fits," he suspected supernatural causes. In order to prove it, he ordered the slave woman Tituba to prepare a witch cake.

Tituba collected urine from the afflicted girls, mixed it with rye meal and ashes, and baked it. Then, she fed the bizarre cake to the family dogs and observed them to see their reaction. According to belief, if the dogs behaved normally, the girls were not bewitched. If, on the other hand, the dogs acted strangely in any way, witches were tormenting the children.

Tituba reported to Parris that the dogs acted unnaturally after eating the witch cake and armed with the necessary evidence, Parris initiated the Salem witch-hunts.

22. Witch Teats

DEVIL'S Marks were important evidence during witch trials. Judges considered evidence of Devil's Marks as proof positive the person with them was a witch. Originally, witch-finders believed Devil's Marks were seals of obedience placed on individual witches by the Devil. However, over time, the belief in the Devil's Mark evolved into the idea that it was an unnatural teat on the body of a witch. Familiar spirits supposedly suckled from these teats.

Witch-finders hired examiners (mostly elderly women) to search suspected witches for teats. If they found loose or dry skin, warts, moles, skin tags, or any other usual growths, on the suspect, they inserted needles or other sharp items into the area. If the suspect did not react, the examiners pronounced that the accused had the Devil's Mark. Once the examiners determined that the accused bore Devil's Marks, exoneration was impossible.

23. Flying Ointment

WITCH-FINDERS generally believed that witches could fly, but not by a mere waive of the Devil's hand. They believed that witches used a special ointment or salve that allowed them to soar above the clouds on broomsticks, tree branches, or poles. At various times witch-finders referred to the potion as "Flying Ointment," "Green Ointment," Magic Salve," "Lycanthropic Ointment," "Hexensalbe" ("Witch Salve"), "Flugsalbe" ("Flying Salve"), and others.

Composition

Few mythical concoctions have a definite recipe, but Flying Ointment has several.

English philosopher and author, Sir Francis Bacon, produced a recipe for Flying Ointment. Bacon's list of ingredients included:

1. "... the fat of children digged out of their graves ..."

The thought of using human body fat in any kind of an ointment seems gruesome. Yet, it has a long history of use. The fact is that from around the beginning of the 16th Century until the mid 20th Century, human body fat was a common ingredient in many ointments and pharmaceuticals.

2. "... the juices of smallage ..."

Smallage is a type of celery that grows in the wild.

3. "... wolfe-bane ..."

Wolf's-bane has a connection to several supernatural myths and receives mention as an ingredient in several supposedly magic recipes. In most of its forms, wolf's-bane is extremely toxic.

4. "... cinque foil ..."

Cinquefoil is a variety of the Potentilla plant.

Bacon wrote that the above ingredients "mingled" with wheat flour would result in Flying Ointment.

Bacon's Flying Ointment recipe was just one of many recorded throughout history. The others included mostly poisonous ingredients such as belladonna, black henbane, hemlock, henbane, jimson weed, mandrake, and wolf's-bane.

One should never try to make Flying Ointment. Every known recipe contains highly toxic ingredients that can kill anyone that swallows or absorbs them through the skin. Fatalities resulting from failed attempts to make Flying Ointment litter history.

One famous case of a person dying while attempting to create Flying Ointment took place in Meiningen, Germany. On April 15, 1895, historian, occultist, and theosophist Carl Kiesewetter died after ingesting the ingredients of the Flying Ointment he was trying to make.

Was Flying Illegal?

Jane Wenham went on trial for witchcraft in Hertford, England on March 4, 1712 (thirty years after the Salem witch trials). Several eyewitnesses testified to seeing Wenham fly. The Judge of the Assize Court hearing the case was Sir John Powell. Powell weighted the testimony, consulted the law, and ruled that flying was not a crime in Great Britain.

24. Pricking Tools

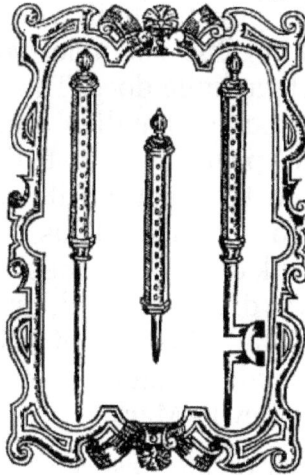

FINDING Devil's Marks was important in convicting witches. Inquisitors developed a definitive method of proving that marks on the body were unnatural. One method as pricking witches.

The belief was that Devil's Marks had no sensitivity and that pricking them would cause the witch no pain. During the many witch-hunts in the 16th and 17th Centuries, examiners used pins, needles, and bodkins (rather long, thin, instruments resembling small daggers used for drawing ribbons through hems or punching holes in cloth), and other sharp objects to prick witches.

Over time, witch-finders created tools to aid them in proving that skin deformities and blemishes were Devil's Marks. Some of these tools were so intimidating that accused witches often confessed rather than enduring the agony they caused.

Some of the pricking tools only appeared to pierce the skin. One example worked in the same way a stage knife does. These fake pricks had hollow wooden handles and retractable points. When pushed against the skin, the point appeared to penetrate it, but in fact, it retreated into handle. Thus, although it appeared to sink deeply into the flesh, the point made no mark, drew no blood, and caused the suspect no pain. This bit of fakery usually convinced the judges that the questionable skin blemish was a Devil's Mark.

Another tool created especially for pricking Devil's Marks was a needle that had one sharp end and one dull end. Examiners pricked "normal" flesh with the sharp end causing pain and drawing blood. Then, using the other end, they pricked suspected Devil's Marks. Of course, the dull end caused no pain and didn't bring blood, The judges then concluded that the blemish must be a Devil's Mark. Apparently, the judges trusted the examiners and did not bother to scrutinize their activities. There are no known instances of judges catching examiners cheating during their pricking tests.

25. Prayer Test

ONE of the most commonly held tenets of witch lore was that a person under the influence of the Devil could not quote scripture without faltering and making mistakes. During many witch trails, particularly in Salem, one of the ordeals inquisitors put suspected witches through was the Prayer Test.

The test was simple, but insidious. The Inquisitors forced the accused to stand before a crowed court and recite a biblical verse, usually the *Lord's Prayer*. Anything other than a perfect recital served as proof that the accused was a witch. The poor, frightened person tried to repeat the prayer from memory before the prying eyes. She knew if she stuttered, or stumbled, or used one word out of place, she would hang.

Perhaps the most important Puritan Minister in New England, Cotton Mather approved of the Prayer Test as a reliable method of detecting witches. Mather wrote a judge:

"I should not be unwilling that an experiment be made whether accused parties can repeat the *Lord's Prayer*, or those other systems of Christianity which, it seems, the devils often make the witches unable to repeat without ridiculous depravations or amputations."

The test was weighted against the accused. Even if the accused had memorized the Bible, they might be unable to speak in public due to nerves. Stage fright notwithstanding, many of the accused were elderly and illiterate. It is little wonder that so many failed to recite the *Lord's Prayer* from memory.

While failing the Prayer Test meant sure conviction, passing it did not ensure acquittal. The accusers at Salem branded Reverend George Burroughs "the King of Witches." Burroughs denied he was a witch, but the court convicted him nonetheless. Standing on the gallows just before his execution, Burroughs recited the Bible flawlessly. However, it did not save his life. The witch-mad leaders in Salem contended that the recital was nothing more than one of the many tricks the Devil played.

Different Versions of the Lord's Prayer

Oddly, the King James Version of the Bible lists the *Lord's Prayer* twice. The two versions of the *Lord's Prayer* differed from each other slightly and it is possible that if a witch repeated the wrong version, the court would have convicted her.

The two versions of the *Lord's Prayer* printed in the King James Version of the Bible follow below.

Matthew 6: 9-13: "... Our Father which art in heaven, Hallowed be thy name. Thy kingdom come, Thy will be done in earth, as it is in heaven. Give us this day our daily bread. And forgive us our debts, as we forgive our debtors.

And lead us not into temptation, but deliver us from evil: For thine is the kingdom, and the power, and the glory, for ever. Amen.

Luke 11: 2-4: "... Our Father which art in heaven, Hallowed be thy name. Thy kingdom come. Thy will be done, as in heaven, so in earth. Give us day by day our daily bread. And forgive us our sins; for we also forgive every one that is indebted to us. And lead us not into temptation; but deliver us from evil."

26. Exhaustion Torture

SLEEP deprivation and walking torture was very effective in enticing confessions from those accused of witchcraft. After about three days of being awake, hallucinations often set in and the will to resist crumbled. The confessions extracted from the accused witches often revealed wildly bizarre and impossible scenes such as flying, transforming into animals, meeting the Devil personally, and taking part in Witch Sabbaths.

Keeping an accused witch moving though walking for many hours hastened exhaustion and led to quicker confessions by the poor, tortured souls.

27. Dunking Test

DUNKING was a punishment for petty crimes and misdemeanors before it became a common witch test. Early on, community officials dunked "disorderly" women, gossips, crooked tradesmen, women that bore illegitimate children, and prostitutes. The point of the punishment was public humiliation.

Over time, witch-finders turned to the well-known method of dunking to identify witches. Sometimes the witch-finders attached suspects to chairs and dunked them, but more often, they made the ordeal more difficult on the accused.

It became common for the authorities to put a witch through a dunking test (also referred to as a "swimming test") by tying the suspect's right thumb to her left big toe. They then tied a rope around her waist and threw her into a deep pond or stream. If the suspect floated, they declared her a witch. If she sank, it proved her innocent. However, suspects often drowned before the witch-finders could pull them out of the water.

The last cases of dunking in England took place in 1808 (Mrs. Ganble) 1809 (Jenny Pipes), and 1817 (Sarah Leeke), respectively. None of the women mentioned faced charges of witchcraft.

Dunking ended in the United States long before it did in England.

SECTION III: THE DEVIL

WITCH-FINDERS made war on supposed witches based on the Puritan interpretation of biblical references to the Devil. This section looks at those beliefs and what the Bible said about the Devil.

28. Who is the Devil?

PARADISE LOST.

PURITANS believed that the Devil and his angels made war against God in Heaven. After his defeat in Heaven, the Devil continued his war on earth. As part of his plan, hen enlisted humans to help him. Most Puritans did not believe the Devil could succeed in overthrowing God's kingdom. Yet, they felt it was their duty to fight against the Prince of Darkness nonetheless. Of course, they could not defeat the Devil directly. Therefore, they contented themselves with defeating his human helpers.

As do most Christians still do, the Puritans believed the Devil was evil incarnate. Once the most beloved of the angels, he rebelled against God and fell from grace. From then on the Devil assumed the role as God's primary adversary.

Puritans held the Devil to be pure evil with no compassion or other redeeming quality. His earthly war was one of terror and murder. The more people he could destroy – allies and enemies alike – the better he liked it.

The Puritans believed that one-third of the angels joined in the Devil's rebellion in Heaven and when God threw the Devil out of Heaven, the rebellious angles went with him and continued the civil war on earth. God promised to punish the Devil and his angels by casting them in the Lake of Fire at the end of time.

An earlier chapter details what confessed witches said the Devil looked like. However, artists often presented the Devil as a more sinister and frightful being than those that claimed to see him did. The artwork often portrayed the Devil as a horned goat or ram with stringy fur and the nose, ears and teeth of a swine.

The Bible often represented the Devil as a serpent, viper, or dragon. The Bible also stated that the Devil had a certain dominion over the earth and was "The god of this world."

The Devil went by many names in the Bible, and later Christians gave him even more. The Puritans used many of these names for the Devil interchangeably. Other of the names came into vogue long after extreme versions of the Puritan sect had passed. Below is a sampling of some of the names associated with the Devil:

Beelzebub: The word translates to "The Lord of Flies," and implies that the Devil is the author of plagues.

Dark Lord: This name was one of several that associated the Devil with darkness. A variant of the name was Prince of Darkness.

Dragon: The Bible often associated the Devil with a powerful, snakelike creature similar to a dragon. Sometimes, the Bible called the Devil a serpent.

The Evil One: The Devil was pure evil and had no qualities worthy of redemption.

The Father of Lies: Jesus said, "I am the truth." The Devil was the opposite. He was the father of lies and the truth was not in him.

God of this world: Several verses of the Bible name the Devil as the god of earth.

Lucifer: Lucifer was the Devil's name before he rebelled against God.

Roaring Lion: The Bible sometimes referred to the Devil as a roaring lion.

Satan: The word Satan, translates to "the Adversary, Accuser, and Prosecutor." It is the most common name used for the Devil.

29. The Bible on the Devil

HUNDREDS of biblical verses refer to the Devil by one name of another. Biblical authors devoted more time to the Devil than they did to almost any other subject.

The witch-finders interpreted many of the verses about the Devil as indictments of witches and incitements to destroy them.

Below is a representative sampling of biblical references to the Devil. These references come from 29 of the 66 books of the King James Version of the Bible.

Genesis 3:1-15: "Now the serpent was more subtle than any beast of the field which the Lord God had made. And he said unto the woman, Yea, hath God said, Ye shall not eat of every tree of the garden? And the woman said unto the serpent, We may eat of the fruit of the trees of the garden: But of the fruit of the tree which is in the midst of the garden, God hath said, Ye shall not eat of it, neither shall ye touch it, lest ye die. And the serpent said unto the woman, Ye shall not surely die: For God doth know that in the day ye eat thereof, then your eyes shall be opened, and ye shall be as gods, knowing good and evil. And when the woman saw that the tree was good for food, and that it was pleasant to the eyes, and a tree to be desired to make one wise, she took of the fruit thereof, and did eat, and gave also unto her husband with her; and he did eat. And the eyes of them both were opened, and they knew that they were naked; and they sewed fig leaves together, and made themselves aprons. And they heard the voice of the Lord God walking in the garden in the cool of the day: and Adam and his wife hid themselves from the presence of the Lord God amongst the trees of the garden. And the Lord God called unto Adam, and said unto him, Where art thou? And he said, I heard thy voice in the garden, and I was afraid, because I was naked; and I hid myself. And he said, Who told thee that thou wast naked? Hast thou eaten of the tree, whereof I commanded thee that thou shouldest not eat? And the man said, The woman whom thou gavest to be with me, she gave me of the tree, and I did eat. And the Lord God said unto the woman, What is this that thou hast done? And the woman said, The serpent beguiled me, and I did eat. And the Lord God said unto the serpent, Because thou hast done this, thou art cursed above all cattle, and above every beast of the field; upon thy belly shalt thou go, and dust shalt thou eat all the days of thy life: And I will put enmity between thee and the woman, and between thy seed and her seed; it shall bruise thy head, and thou shalt bruise his heel."

1 Samuel 16:14: "But the Spirit of the Lord departed from Saul, and an evil spirit from the Lord troubled him."

1 Kings 22:21-22: "And there came forth a spirit, and stood before the Lord, and said, I will persuade him. And the Lord said unto him, Wherewith? And he said, I will go forth, and I will be a lying spirit in the mouth of all his prophets. And he said, Thou shalt persuade him, and prevail also: go forth, and do so."

1 Chronicles 21:1: "And Satan stood up against Israel, and provoked David to number Israel."

Job 1:6-12: "Now there was a day when the sons of God came to present themselves before then Lord, and Satan came also among them. And the Lord said unto Satan, Whence comest thou? Then Satan answered the Lord, and said, From going to and fro in the earth, and from walking up and down in it. And the Lord said unto Satan, Hast thou considered my servant Job, that there is none like him in the earth, a perfect and an upright man, one that feareth God, and escheweth evil? Then Satan answered the Lord, and said, Doth Job fear God for nought? Hast not thou made an hedge about him, and about his house, and about all that he hath on every side? thou hast blessed the work of his hands, and his substance is increased in the land. But put forth thine hand now, and touch all that he hath, and he will curse thee to thy face. And the Lord said unto Satan, Behold, all that he hath is in thy power; only upon himself put not forth thine hand. So Satan went forth from the presence of the Lord."

Job 2:4-7: "And Satan answered the Lord, and said, Skin for skin, yea, all that a man hath will he give for his life. But put forth thine hand now, and touch his bone and his flesh, and he will curse thee to thy face. And the Lord said unto Satan, Behold, he is in thine hand; but save his life. So went Satan forth from the presence of the Lord, and smote Job with sore boils from the sole of his foot unto his crown."

Psalm 21:11: "For they intended evil against thee: they imagined a mischievous device, which they are not able to perform."

Psalm 91:3, 11-12: "Surely he shall deliver thee from the snare of the fowler, and from the noisome pestilence. ... For he shall give his angels charge over thee, to keep thee in all thy ways. They shall bear thee up in their hands, lest thou dash thy foot against a stone."

Isaiah 14:12-15: "How art thou fallen from heaven, O Lucifer, son of the morning! how art thou cut down to the ground, which didst weaken the nations! For thou hast said in thine heart, I will ascend into heaven, I will exalt my throne above the stars of God: I will sit also upon the mount of the congregation, in the sides of the north: I will ascend above the heights of the clouds; I will be like the most High. Yet thou shalt be brought down to hell, to the sides of the pit."

Zechariah 3:1-2: "And he shewed me Joshua the high priest standing before the angel of the Lord, and Satan standing at his right hand to resist him. And the Lord said unto Satan, The Lord rebuke thee, O Satan; even the Lord that hath chosen Jerusalem rebuke thee: is not this a brand plucked out of the fire?"

Matthew 4:1-11: "Then was Jesus led up of the Spirit into the wilderness to be tempted of the devil. And when he had fasted forty days and forty nights, he was afterward an hungred. And when the tempter came to him, he said, If thou be the Son of God, command that these stones be made bread. But he answered and said, It is written, Man shall not live by bread alone, but by every word that proceedeth out of the mouth of God. Then the devil taketh him up into the holy city, and setteth him on a pinnacle of the temple, And saith unto him, If thou be the Son of God, cast thyself down: for it is written, He shall give his angels charge concerning thee: and in their hands they shall bear thee up, lest at any time thou dash thy foot against a stone. Jesus said unto him, It is written again, Thou shalt not tempt the Lord thy God. Again, the devil taketh him up into an exceeding high mountain, and sheweth him all the kingdoms of the world, and the glory of them; And saith unto him, All these things will I give thee, if thou wilt fall down and worship me. Then saith Jesus unto him, Get thee hence, Satan: for it is written, Thou shalt worship the Lord thy God, and him only shalt thou serve. Then the devil leaveth him, and, behold, angels came and ministered unto him."

Matthew 8:28-33: "And when he was come to the other side into the country of the Gergesenes, there met him two possessed with devils, coming out of the tombs, exceeding fierce, so that no man might pass by that way. And, behold, they cried out, saying, What have we to do with thee, Jesus, thou Son of God? art thou come hither to torment us before the time? And there was a good way off from them an herd of many swine feeding. So the devils besought him, saying, If thou cast us out, suffer us to go away into the herd of swine. And he said unto them, Go. And when they were come out, they went into the herd of swine: and, behold, the whole herd of swine ran violently down a steep place into the sea, and perished in the waters. And they that kept them fled, and went their ways into the city, and told every thing, and what was befallen to the possessed of the devils."

Matthew 10:1: "And when he had called unto him his twelve disciples, he gave them power against unclean spirits, to cast them out, and to heal all manner of sickness and all manner of disease."

Matthew 12:24-28: "But when the Pharisees heard it, they said, This fellow doth not cast out devils, but by Beelzebub the prince of the devils. And Jesus knew their thoughts, and said unto them, Every kingdom divided against itself is brought to desolation; and every city or house divided against itself shall not stand: And if Satan cast out Satan, he is divided against himself; how shall then his kingdom stand? And if I by Beelzebub cast out devils, by whom do your children cast them out? therefore they shall be your judges. But if I cast out devils by the Spirit of God, then the kingdom of God is come unto you."

Matthew 13:4, 19, 25, 28, 29-39: "And when he sowed, some seeds fell by the way side, and the fowls came and devoured them up: ... When any one heareth the word of the kingdom, and understandeth it not, then cometh the wicked one, and catcheth away that which was sown in his heart. This is he which received seed by the way side. ... But while men slept, his enemy came and sowed tares among the wheat, and went his way. ... He said unto them, An enemy hath done this. The servants said unto him, Wilt thou then that we go and gather them up? The field is the world; the good seed are the children of the kingdom; but the tares are the children of the wicked one; The enemy that sowed them is the devil; the harvest is the end of the world; and the reapers are the angels."

Matthew 16:23: "But he turned, and said unto Peter, Get thee behind me, Satan: thou art an offence unto me: for thou savourest not the things that be of God, but those that be of men."

Matthew 17:15, 18: "Lord, have mercy on my son: for he is lunatick, and sore vexed: for ofttimes he falleth into the fire, and oft into the water. ... And Jesus rebuked the devil; and he departed out of him: and the child was cured from that very hour."

Matthew 25:41: "Then shall he say also unto them on the left hand, Depart from me, ye cursed, into everlasting fire, prepared for the devil and his angels:"

Mark 3:14-15: "And he ordained twelve, that they should be with him, and that he might send them forth to preach, And to have power to heal sicknesses, and to cast out devils:"

Mark 16:17: "And these signs shall follow them that believe; In my name shall they cast out devils; they shall speak with new tongues;"

Luke 8:29-33: "For he had commanded the unclean spirit to come out of the man. For oftentimes it had caught him: and he was kept bound with chains and in fetters; and he brake the bands, and was driven of the devil into the wilderness.) And Jesus asked him, saying, What is thy name? And he said, Legion: because many devils were entered into him. And they besought him that he would not command them to go out into the deep. And there was there an herd of many swine feeding on the mountain: and they besought him that he would suffer them to enter into them. And he suffered them. Then went the devils out of the man, and entered into the swine: and the herd ran violently down a steep place into the lake, and were choked."

Luke 9:39-42: "And, behold, a man of the company cried out, saying, Master, I beseech thee, look upon my son: for he is mine only child. And, lo, a spirit taketh him, and he suddenly crieth out; and it teareth him that he foameth again, and bruising him hardly departeth from him. And I besought thy disciples to cast him out; and they could not. And Jesus answering said, O faithless and perverse generation, how long shall I be with you, and suffer you? Bring thy son hither. And as he was yet a coming, the devil threw him down, and tare him. And Jesus rebuked the unclean spirit, and healed the child, and delivered him again to his father."

Luke 10:17-18: "And the seventy returned again with joy, saying, Lord, even the devils are subject unto us through thy name. And he said unto them, I beheld Satan as lightning fall from heaven."

Luke 11:15, 20-22: "But some of them said, He casteth out devils through Beelzebub the chief of the devils. ... But if I with the finger of God cast out devils, no doubt the kingdom of God is come upon you. When a strong man armed keepeth his palace, his goods are in peace: But when a stronger than he shall come upon him, and overcome him, he taketh from him all his armour wherein he trusted, and divideth his spoils."

Luke 13:32: "And he said unto them, Go ye, and tell that fox, Behold, I cast out devils, and I do cures to day and to morrow, and the third day I shall be perfected."

Luke 22:3: "Then entered Satan into Judas surnamed Iscariot, being of the number of the twelve."

Luke 22:31: "And the Lord said, Simon, Simon, behold, Satan hath desired to have you, that he may sift you as wheat:"

John 6:70: "Jesus answered them, Have not I chosen you twelve, and one of you is a devil?"

John 8:44: "Ye are of your father the devil, and the lusts of your father ye will do. He was a murderer from the beginning, and abode not in the truth, because there is no truth in him.

When he speaketh a lie, he speaketh of his own: for he is a liar, and the father of it."

John 10:12: "But he that is an hireling, and not the shepherd, whose own the sheep are not, seeth the wolf coming, and leaveth the sheep, and fleeth: and the wolf catcheth them, and scattereth the sheep."

John 10:20-21: "And many of them said, He hath a devil, and is mad; why hear ye him? Others said, These are not the words of him that hath a devil. Can a devil open the eyes of the blind?"

John 13:2: "And supper being ended, the devil having now put into the heart of Judas Iscariot, Simon's son, to betray him;"

John 14:30: "Hereafter I will not talk much with you: for the prince of this world cometh, and hath nothing in me."

Acts 5:3: "But Peter said, Ananias, why hath Satan filled thine heart to lie to the Holy Ghost, and to keep back part of the price of the land?"

Acts 13:10: "And said, O full of all subtilty and all mischief, thou child of the devil, thou enemy of all righteousness, wilt thou not cease to pervert the right ways of the Lord?"

Acts 19:16: "And the man in whom the evil spirit was leaped on them, and overcame them, and prevailed against them, so that they fled out of that house naked and wounded."

Romans 16:20: "And the God of peace shall bruise Satan under your feet shortly. The grace of our Lord Jesus Christ be with you. Amen."

1 Corinthians 5:5: "To deliver such an one unto Satan for the destruction of the flesh, that the spirit may be saved in the day of the Lord Jesus."

1 Corinthians 10:21: "Ye cannot drink the cup of the Lord, and the cup of devils: ye cannot be partakers of the Lord's table, and of the table of devils."

2 Corinthians 2:11: "Lest Satan should get an advantage of us: for we are not ignorant of his devices."

2 Corinthians 4:4: "In whom the god of this world hath blinded the minds of them which believe not, lest the light of the glorious gospel of Christ, who is the image of God, should shine unto them."

2 Corinthians 11:3, 14: "But I fear, lest by any means, as the serpent beguiled Eve through his subtilty, so your minds should be corrupted from the simplicity that is in Christ. ... And no marvel; for Satan himself is transformed into an angel of light."

Ephesians 2:2: "Wherein in time past ye walked according to the course of this world, according to the prince of the power of the air, the spirit that now worketh in the children of disobedience:"

Ephesians 4:27: "Neither give place to the devil."

Ephesians 6:11-16: "Put on the whole armour of God, that ye may be able to stand against the wiles of the devil. For we wrestle not against flesh and blood, but against principalities, against powers, against the rulers of the darkness of this world, against spiritual wickedness in high places. Wherefore take unto you the whole armour of God, that ye may be able to withstand in the evil day, and having done all, to stand. Stand therefore, having your loins girt about with truth, and having on the breastplate of righteousness; And your feet shod with the preparation of the gospel of peace; Above all, taking the shield of faith, wherewith ye shall be able to quench all the fiery darts of the wicked."

Colossians 2:15: "And having spoiled principalities and powers, he made a shew of them openly, triumphing over them in it."

1 Thessalonians 2:18: "Wherefore we would have come unto you, even I Paul, once and again; but Satan hindered us."

1 Thessalonians 3:5: "For this cause, when I could no longer forbear, I sent to know your faith, lest by some means the tempter have tempted you, and our labour be in vain."

2 Thessalonians 2:9: "Even him, whose coming is after the working of Satan with all power and signs and lying wonders,"

1 Timothy 3:6-7: "Not a novice, lest being lifted up with pride he fall into the condemnation of the devil. Moreover he must have a good report of them which are without; lest he fall into reproach and the snare of the devil."

1 Timothy 4:1-2: "Now the Spirit speaketh expressly, that in the latter times some shall depart from the faith, giving heed to seducing spirits, and doctrines of devils; Speaking lies in hypocrisy; having their conscience seared with a hot iron;"

1 Timothy 5:15: "For some are already turned aside after Satan."

2 Timothy 2:26: "And that they may recover themselves out of the snare of the devil, who are taken captive by him at his will."

Hebrews 2:14-15: "Forasmuch then as the children are partakers of flesh and blood, he also himself likewise took part of the same; that through death he might destroy him that had the power of death, that is, the devil; And deliver them who through fear of death were all their lifetime subject to bondage."

James 2:19: "Thou believest that there is one God; thou doest well: the devils also believe, and tremble."

James 3:14-15: "But if ye have bitter envying and strife in your hearts, glory not, and lie not against the truth. This wisdom descendeth not from above, but is earthly, sensual, devilish."

James 4:7: "Submit yourselves therefore to God. Resist the devil, and he will flee from you."

1 Peter 5:8-9: "Be sober, be vigilant; because your adversary the devil, as a roaring lion, walketh about, seeking whom he may devour:
9 Whom resist stedfast in the faith, knowing that the same afflictions are accomplished in your brethren that are in the world."

2 Peter 2:4: "For if God spared not the angels that sinned, but cast them down to hell, and delivered them into chains of darkness, to be reserved unto judgment;"

1 John 2:13: "I write unto you, fathers, because ye have known him that is from the beginning. I write unto you, young men, because ye have overcome the wicked one. I write unto you, little children, because ye have known the Father."

1 John 3:8, 10, 12: "He that committeth sin is of the devil; for the devil sinneth from the beginning. For this purpose the Son of God was manifested, that he might destroy the works of the devil. ... In this the children of God are manifest, and the children of the devil: whosoever doeth not righteousness is not of God, neither he that loveth not his brother. ... Not as Cain, who was of that wicked one, and slew his brother. And wherefore slew he him? Because his own works were evil, and his brother's righteous."

1 John 5:19: "And we know that we are of God, and the whole world lieth in wickedness."

Jude 1:6: "And the angels which kept not their first estate, but left their own habitation, he hath reserved in everlasting chains under darkness unto the judgment of the great day."

Revelation 2:13: "I know thy works, and where thou dwellest, even where Satan's seat is: and thou holdest fast my name, and hast not denied my faith, even in those days wherein Antipas was my faithful martyr, who was slain among you, where Satan dwelleth."

Revelation 12:10-17: "And there was war in heaven: Michael and his angels fought against the dragon; and the dragon fought and his angels, And prevailed not; neither was their place found any more in heaven. And the great dragon was cast out, that old serpent, called the Devil, and Satan, which deceiveth the whole world: he was cast out into the earth, and his angels were cast out with him. And I heard a loud voice saying in heaven, Now is come salvation, and strength, and the kingdom of our God, and the power of his Christ: for the accuser of our brethren is cast down, which accused them before our God day and night. And they overcame him by the blood of the Lamb, and by the word of their testimony; and they loved not their lives unto the death. Therefore rejoice, ye heavens, and ye that dwell in them. Woe to the inhabiters of the earth and of the sea! for the devil is come down unto you, having great wrath, because he knoweth that he hath but a short time. And when the dragon saw that he was cast unto the earth, he persecuted the woman which brought forth the man child. And to the woman were given two wings of a great eagle, that she might fly into the wilderness, into her place, where she is nourished for a time, and times, and half a time, from the face of the serpent. And the serpent cast out of his mouth water as a flood after the woman, that he might cause her to be carried away of the flood. And the earth helped the woman, and the earth opened her mouth, and swallowed up the flood which the dragon cast out of his mouth. And the dragon was wroth with the woman, and went to make war with the remnant of her seed, which keep the commandments of God, and have the testimony of Jesus Christ.

Revelation 16:13-14: "And I saw three unclean spirits like frogs come out of the mouth of the dragon, and out of the mouth of the beast, and out of the mouth of the false prophet. For they are the spirits of devils, working miracles, which go forth unto the kings of the earth and of the whole world, to gather them to the battle of that great day of God Almighty."

Revelation 20:2: "And he laid hold on the dragon, that old serpent, which is the Devil, and Satan, and bound him a thousand years,"

Revelation 20:7-10: "And when the thousand years are expired, Satan shall be loosed out of his prison, And when the thousand years are expired, Satan shall be loosed out of his prison, And shall go out to deceive the nations which are in the four quarters of the earth, Gog, and Magog, to gather them together to battle: the number of whom is as the sand of the sea. And they went up on the breadth of the earth, and compassed the camp of the saints about, and the beloved city: and fire came down from God out of heaven, and devoured them. And the devil that deceived them was cast into the lake of fire and brimstone, where the beast and the false prophet are, and shall be tormented day and night for ever and ever."

Conclusion

THE Court of Assizes at Norfolk adjourned without making a determination on what to do with Hopkins and his witch-finding cadre. However, he had not convinced them of his purity. By the time the court resumed its deliberations, Hopkins had retired to Manningtree, leaving the question moot.

Hopkins evidently felt he needed to broadcast the contents of his testimony to the public at large. Soon after the hearing ended, he published, a pamphlet called *The Discovery of Witches*. In it, he described and defended some of his methods.

While Hopkins publicly declared victory in his encounter with the judges, he abandoned his witch-finding career immediately after testifying before the Court of Assizes. The evidence is that he retired due to illness. But fear that the court might punish him may also have been a factor in Hopkins giving up witch finding.

Hopkins died, probably of tuberculosis, on August 12, 1647. He was about 27.

Although Hopkins was gone and memory of him as a man faded quickly, his legacy of torture and abuse continued in both Europe and in the New World for decades. Whether purposely, or by happenstance, Puritans in Massachusetts and other parts of New England employed many of the witch-finding methods popularized by Hopkins. Some used his methods as if they were following a demented playbook.

There are many, many examples of North American colonists applying exactly the same type of tortures that Hopkins had employed nearly half a century before. One excellent example is the treatment of the slave woman Tituba. Judge John Hathorne questioned Tituba about her alleged part in the witch cult in Salem. She started by telling the judge that Samuel Parris had beaten her, ordered her to confess, and promised to kill her if she didn't. Tituba then confessed to being a witch and implicated others as well.

The fact that Tituba stated that her confession came only after her torture did not move Judge Hathorne. He accepted her testimony as true and used it as a basis to interrogate other accused witches. Some of those witches died based on Tituba's tainted confession.

Selected Sources

Bernard, Richard (author), Brett Warren (editor). *A Guide to Grand-Jury Men in Modern English* (1627). CreateSpace, 2017.

Boyer, Paul S. and Stephen Nissenbaum, editors. *Salem-Village Witchcraft: A Documentary Record of Local Conflict in Colonial New England.* Boston: Northeastern University Press, 1972.

Cabell, Craig. *Witchfinder General: The Biography of Matthew Hopkins.* Stroud, United Kingdom: Sutton Publishing, 2006.

Campbell Thompson, R. *Semitic Magic: Its Origins and Development.* New York: Weiser Books, 2000.

Deacon, Richard. *Matthew Hopkins: Witch Finder General.* London: Frederick Muller, 1976.

Evans, G. Blakemore (1997). *The Riverside Shakespeare* (2nd ed.). Boston: Mifflin, 1997.

Gammon, CL. *A Laughing Witch: Hanging Susannah Martin.* Lafayette, Tennessee: Createspace, 2018.

Gammon, CL. *Dixie Witches: 9 True Southern Witch Trials.* Lafayette, Tennessee: Createspace, 2017.

Gammon, CL. *Salem Sends Its First Witch to the Gallows.* Lafayette, Tennessee: Createspace, 2017.

Gammon, CL. *The Queen and King of Hell in Salem.* Lafayette, Tennessee: Createspace, 2020.

Gammon, CL. *The Witches of Salem, In Their Own Words.* Lafayette, Tennessee: Createspace, 2020.

Gaskill, Malcolm. *Witchfinders: A Seventeenth-Century English Tragedy.* Cambridge, Massachusetts: Harvard University Press, 2007.

Geis, Gilbert and Ivan Bunn. *A Trial of Witches: A Seventeenth-Century Witchcraft Prosecution.* Milton Park, United Kingdom: Routledge Publishing, 1997.

Hansen, Harold A. *The Witch's Garden.* Newbury Port, Massachusetts: Unity Press, 1978.

Hopkins, Matthew. *The Discovery of Witches.* (1647). CreateSpace, 2013, reprint.

King James, G. B. Harrison (editor) *Daemonologie.*, New York: E. P. Dutton, 1924, reprint of the 1597 version.

Lewis, James R., Evelyn Dorothy Oliver, and Kelle S. Sisung (Editor) *Angels A to Z.* Detroit: Visible Ink Press, 1996.

Mack, Dinah and Carol K. Mack. *A Field Guide to Demons, Fairies, Fallen Angels and Other Subversive Spirits.* New York: Henry Holt and Company, LLC, 1999.

Masello, Robert. *Fallen Angels and Spirits of The Dark.* New York: The Berkley Publishing Group, 2004.

Notestein, Wallace. *A History of Witchcraft In England from 1558 to 1718*. New York: Russell & Russell, 1911.

Russell, Jeffrey Burton, *A History of Witchcraft*. London: Thames & Hudson, 1981.

Russell, Jeffrey Burton. *Witchcraft in The Middle Ages*. Ithaca, New York: Cornell University Press, 1972.

Seth, Robert. *Children Against Witches*. London: Robert Hale Co., 1969.

Stephens, Walter. *Demon Lovers*. Chicago: The University of Chicago Press, 2002

Thomas, Keith. *Religion and the Decline of Magic – Studies in Popular Beliefs in Sixteenth and Seventeenth Century England*. New York: Penguin Books, 1971.

About the Author

CL Gammon has had a life-long fascination with American history and with the written word. These joint fascinations have led to his becoming an award-winning author of more than sixty books. Gammon, who studied Political Science at Tennessee Technological University and History and Government at Hillsdale College, has entertained and educated readers for decades. Several universities, including the State University of New York and the University of Akron, have utilized his books as course material. In addition, articles written by Gammon have appeared in more than a dozen national and regional publications. Gammon has also written feature stories for his hometown newspaper, the *Macon County Times*. Gammon lives in Lafayette, Tennessee.

Index

www.ingramcontent.com/pod-product-compliance
Lightning Source LLC
Chambersburg PA
CBHW060301050426
42448CB00009B/1717